Pig in a poke

D0811239

PIG IN A POKE

PIG IN A POKE

Grange
BOOKS

First published by Grange Books in 2003

an imprint of Grange Books PLC
The Grange
Kingsnorth Industrial Estate
Hoo nr Rochester
Kent
UK
ME3 9ND
www.grangebooks.co.uk

422

ISBN - 1840136251

Page make up by Penny Mills
Printed and bound in Thailand

INTRODUCTION

Most of us will, on a daily basis, pepper our conversation with phrases and sayings that we have collected from the English language that has surrounded us from our infancy. We may use them automatically because they are so familiar we do so without really thinking about them, or consciously employ them to sum up precisely what we wish to say in a way we would find hard to better. Sometimes we just enjoy repeating them because they are colourful, even bizarre, and help to grab a listener's attention.

Occasionally we may stop in our verbal tracks and wonder just how a certain saying came into being and what it originally meant before its literal meaning became obscure to us. Why use the expression 'kicking the bucket' to mean 'dying', or speak of 'getting our ducks in a row' when trying to be organized, or refer to a 'nine days' wonder' as being 'a flash in the pan'?

The hope is that the answer to these and hundreds of similar enquiries will be found in the pages that follow. Or, to put it another way, we hope that *Pig in a Poke* will 'let the cat out of the bag' when you want to know why you're 'talking turkey'.

Above and below the salt

At medieval feasts, where you sat in relation to the salt-cellar was highly significant. The custom was to place a large cellar in the centre of the table for communal use. The most esteemed guests and members of the household would sit between the salt and the host, 'above the salt', and those of less importance sat 'below the salt'. In time, the expression became verbal shorthand for indicating a person's perceived status in society.

Acid test

The 'acid test' is the process that proves something beyond doubt and the expression comes from the test used to confirm whether or not a metal is gold – for gold is not affected by the majority of acids. The one that it is certain to react with is a mixture of concentrated nitric and hydrochloric acid, In medieval alchemy this was given the Latin name Aqua Regia, meaning 'royal water', because it dissolved the king of metals.

All at sixes and sevens

One of several expressions describing a state of confusion, or an inability to reach an agreement, this has a curious ancestry. While it may be associated with the throwing of dice, there is tradition based in history that links it to a dispute that took place towards the end of the fifteenth century between two of the livery companies in the City of London. The Merchant Taylors and the Skinners received their charters within a few days of each other early in the fourteenth century. However, they failed to agree which company should be sixth and which seventh in the order of companies as they processed through the city. The matter was resolved by agreeing that they would take it in turns, with one company occupying sixth place one year and the other occupying it the following year. Once this had been resolved it could be said that they at least were no longer 'at sixes and sevens'.

All his geese are swans

There are echoes of the tale of the Ugly Duckling in this saying, although it does not convey the happy ending of the nursery story. The swan was, and remains, a royal bird both on the water and on the table. Only those of the highest station had leave to dine on swan, while geese were popularly consumed by one and all.

'All his geese are swans' has two related meanings, both of which point to over-inflated opinions on the part of those who see the world through rose-tinted glasses. The saying could be ascribed to anyone who overestimates; the same is true of the man whose children are paragons in his own eyes and who remains firmly convinced that everything he does is superlative.

The saying is also used in its reverse form: 'All your swans are geese'. This is the inevitable retort when fine promises or boastful expectations are proved to be ill-founded.

All my eye and Betty Martin

This curious expression, which now means that something is all nonsense, has an uncertain origin. Traditionally it is thought to be the garbled version among British sailors of the prayer of request heard abroad, 'O mihi, beate Martine', which means 'Oh grant me, blessed St Martin'. 'It's all my eye . . .' is an older saying.

All's grist that comes to my mill

Grist is the term used for a quantity of corn to be ground by a miller at any one time. When all the grist is converted to flour, nothing is left over and allowed to go to waste. Used figuratively, this saying carries the meaning that the speaker can take advantage of anything and is capable of making use of anything or any opportunity presented.

All ship-shape and Bristol fashion

In the days of sail when Bristol was one of the largest ports in England, it had a reputation for efficiency. That has been passed down in this popular turn of phrase which describes being totally prepared and ready for an undertaking, just as a well-organized ship would be prior to setting out on a voyage.

An apple a day keeps the doctor away

This well-known piece of dietary advice may be an early forerunner of the current belief among dieticians that our health improves when we eat five portions of fresh fruit and vegetables every day. In 1866 a proverb quoted in *Notes & Queries*, ran:

> Eat an apple on going to bed,
> And you'll keep the doctor from earning his bread.

An Englishman's home is his castle

A saying dear to the heart of every Englishman, it was Sir Edward Coke, the Lord Chief Justice from 1613–17, who enshrined the principle in his *Institutes*, which are considered to be a legal classic. Coke was seen as a great defender of the common law against the right of the Crown and wrote: 'The house of every man is to him as his castle and fortresse, as well as for his defence against injury and violence, as for his repose.'

The reference was to the fact that a bailiff should not have, and still does not have, the right to break into a man's home. But in modern times, an Englishman's 'castle' is not quite as inviolable as Coke envisaged it. Nowadays, under certain conditions, a number of public authorities have the right of entry to a private house – and in extreme cases can even destroy it, under the terms of certain compulsory purchase orders.

An axe to grind

Anyone with an axe to grind offers help or friendship with an eye to furthering some personal interest or advantage. As a boy the American statesman Benjamin Franklin had first-hand experience of someone with 'an axe to grind'. Persuaded by flattery, the young Franklin turned the heavy grindstone while the owner of the axe sharpened his blade. When the job was finished the man with the axe laughed at Franklin for his foolishness. For the rest of his life Franklin was suspicious that those who flattered him might merely be others 'with an axe to grind'.

Apple-pie order

For something to be in apple-pie order everything needs to be perfectly arranged in its proper place, neat and in order. Cooking, delicious as the outcome may be, has nothing to do with this. Its origins most likely lie in two Old French expressions: *cap à pied*, which came from medieval warfare and meant fully armed from 'head to foot'; and *nappes pliées*, the French for 'folded linen', bringing ideas of neatly folded, crisply ironed sheets and other linen.

As cool as a cucumber

The humble cucumber was already being grown in England in the sixteenth century but enjoyed a far from enviable reputation. Cucumbers were thought to have a dampening effect on lust, and the first version of the simile, 'as cold as a cucumber', was applied particularly to women. In 1732, the playwright John Gay referred to 'as cool as a cucumber' as 'a new simile' and it eventually took over from the original expression. It is used to describe someone who is composed and self-possessed.

Curiously, 'cucumber' was also a slang name for a tailor, and 'cucumber-time' was from mid-July to mid-September (the cucumber growing season), when traditionally tailors' workshops were quiet and when tailors had leave to play.

Ash before oak

One of the most widely-quoted weather proverbs foretells what the summer will be like from the time that leaves start appearing on two of our native hardwood trees: the ash and the oak. This is known in a number of rhyming versions, of which this is one:

> If the oak be out before the ash
> There'll only be a little splash;
> If the ash be out before the oak
> Then there'll be a regular soak.

As sure as eggs is eggs

Ungrammatical though it may be, this expression is a long-winded way of saying something is a certainty. It has been suggested that the original expression was the algebraic formula 'x is x', and that, in common use, it was transformed by those whose mathematical knowledge was poor.

As the crow flies

Traditionally crows have been believed to fly back to their nests using the most direct line of flight and the saying became popular from the early nineteenth century, when a greater mobility began in society, as an indication of the shortest distance between two points.

Strictly speaking, it is the rook rather than the carrion crow which flies in a direct line back to its nest, though country people have been less concerned with a crow's 'flight path' than with its altitude. High-flying crows, returning in the evening to their nests, have long been regarded as a portent of fine weather the following day, whereas crows taking a low-level route home in the evening suggest that the next day will be wet.

As thin as Banbury cheese

The Oxfordshire market town of Banbury, famous in children's folklore for the nursery rhyme 'Ride a cock-horse to Banbury Cross', is also well known for Banbury cakes, spiced turnovers that were once a speciality of the town, and Banbury cheese.

The latter is a type of rich milk cheese, which when ready for consumption is about one inch thick, making it considerably slimmer than most English cheeses.

By way of comparison, then, to be 'as thin as Banbury cheese' is to be very thin indeed.

As well be hanged for a sheep as a lamb

It was only in the nineteenth century that the theft of a sheep or a lamb in some parts of the country ceased to be punishable by death. Two centuries earlier the saying 'as well be hanged for a sheep as for a lamb' was already a much-quoted proverb, implying that if the consequences are the same, it is worthwhile aiming for something of higher value than of lower.

As it developed, the saying broadened in meaning, advising

against stopping at half-measures, but encouraging boldness of endeavour, particularly when an illicit enterprise was being undertaken.

As you sow, so you reap

The image of the sower is drawn upon in a number of instances in Holy Scripture and it is in St Paul's letter to the Galatians that this familiar saying is rooted: 'Be not deceived; God is not mocked: for whatsoever a man soweth, that also shall he reap. For he that soweth to his flesh shall of the flesh reap corruption; but he that soweth to the Spirit shall of the Spirit reap life everlasting. And let us not be weary in well doing: for in due season we shall reap, if we faint not.'

The inference here is clear: the manner of actions has a direct influence on their outcome. In other words, if you conduct yourself well, good will follow from what you do and vice versa.

At loggerheads

People 'at loggerheads' with each other are in a state of disagreement. A 'logger' is the name given to the heavy wooden block once used to hobble horses to prevent them from straying. As an extension of this a 'loggerhead' equates to a 'blockhead' and perhaps to be 'at loggerheads' with someone was seen by others as being locked in a state in which neither would give way and both parties were mindlessly obstinate.

At the eleventh hour

Although the last of the labourers hired in the parable of the labourers in St Matthew's gospel were hired at 'the eleventh hour', the phrase has taken on a distinctly martial tone since the signing of the armistice which ended the First World War at the eleventh hour of the eleventh day of the eleventh month of 1918. In its biblical, and more usual, sense, 'the eleventh hour' has become synonymous with 'at the last minute'.

At the end of your tether

Most of us at some time have experienced the intense exasperation which comes when our patience and self-control reach their limit and we get to the point of total despair and utter frustration, which, to put it another way, leaves us 'at the end of our tether'.

The analogy in this well-used turn of phrase is to an animal left to graze, but secured by a rope, or tether, rather than being allowed to roam freely. Such an animal can graze as far as its tether will let it move from the point where the tether is secured. Once it reaches the end of the tether, it cannot move further. Fettered like this, the grazing animal might perhaps experience the frustration which has given rise to the expression.

Back to square one

'Back to square one' originated from a game of some sort; the question is which game precisely. There are two principal contenders: football and Snakes and Ladders. The argument in favour of football dates from the early days of radio commentaries of football matches given by the BBC. To help listeners follow the passage of play, the *Radio Times* printed a map of the football pitch divided into numbered squares, which commentators called out as play moved from square to square. When the ball went into 'square one', the argument runs that the commentary went 'back to square one'. The weakness in this line of thought is that there is no reason why 'square one' should have been the 'starting point'. After a stoppage play could have recommenced from any square on the pitch, which might or might not have been 'square one'. The 'Snakes and Ladders' theory does offer a logical return to 'square one', or close to it. Any players unlucky enough to land on one of the long snakes running from near the top of the board, risks sliding back down almost to the very beginning, or 'back to square one'.

Baker's dozen

A 'baker's dozen' contains thirteen items as opposed to the familiar twelve. This dates from the time when bakers were subject to heavy fines if they served under-weight bread. To avoid this danger, bakers provided a surplus number of loaves, the thirteenth loaf in the dozen being called the vantage loaf.

Barracking

Most people know what 'barracking' is when they hear it, but putting an explanation to how the word came into being isn't as easy. One thing that is certain is that 'barracking' first came into regular usage in Australia towards the end of the nineteenth century as an expression that summed up the noisy jeering by spectators at things that displeased them at football and cricket matches. There is an Australian aboriginal word *borak* which means 'fun' or 'chaffing', which may have been combined with the Cockney word *barrakin* meaning 'a jumble of words'. The origin of 'barracking' may lie in the alliance of these two. However, there is an equally valid geographical reason associated with football games played close to the Victoria Barracks in Melbourne. The rough crowds that came to watch these games were known as 'barrackers'.

Barbara and her barns

When a thick band of cloud blankets the western sky with smaller cloud bands above and below it, this is colourfully referred to as Barbara and her barns [bairns, children].

This is an obscure reference to St Barbara, who was saved from execution by her own father when he was struck dead by a bolt of lightning just as he was about to chop off his daughter's head. Saved by this unexpected intervention, St Barbara became associated with the power to control thunderstorms and was therefore invoked as a protectress against them.

Barking up the wrong tree

This descriptive turn of phrase implying wasted or misdirected effort derives from the North American method of hunting racoons. Traditionally racoons were hunted in the dark and dogs were used to identify the trees up which racoons had escaped. It was not uncommon for dogs to be mistaken in the dark, barking up the wrong tree when the racoon had found refuge elsewhere.

Bean feast

Today's annual outing or special occasion dates from an earlier feast given once a year by an employer for his or her employees. At many bean feasts held at the end of the year, a bean goose was commonly served. This large grey bird arrives in England in the autumn and gets its name from the bean-shaped mark on its bill. Beans themselves were frequently served as an important addition to the 'bean feast'.

Beating about the bush

The hunt, the chase and latterly the shoot have been features of rural life since ancient times and it is from these that the saying 'beating about the bush' comes. In the sporting field, game of all sorts takes refuge in thickets. Huntsmen in pursuit of game, whether using dogs, nets, bows and arrows, or shotguns, always employ great caution in approaching undergrowth or dense woodland where their quarry may be hiding. When the hunters are in place and ready, teams of beaters surround the 'bush' and then move through it systematically, driving the game towards the waiting hunters. From this, the saying 'beating about the bush' has adopted a wider meaning in which it is applied to approaching a subject cautiously and in a roundabout way, as opposed to tackling it head on.

Before you can say Jack Robinson

There are two likely candidates for the identity of the original Jack Robinson. The first was the late eighteenth-century English politician, John Robinson, who was accused of bribery on the floor of the House of Commons. When his accuser, the playwright and MP Richard Brinsley Sheridan, was asked to name the member of the government under suspicion, he looked directly across at Robinson and replied, 'I could name him as soon as I could say Jack Robinson.' The second was the central character in Thomas Hudson's popular composition *Jack Robinson* which appeared at the beginning of the nineteenth century. Returning home to find his beloved married to another, he went back to the sea 'afore you could say Jack Robinson'. Either way, 'before you can say Jack Robinson' has been passed down over nearly two centuries as another way of saying 'immediately', 'in an instant'.

Best bib and tucker

This expression is still recognized as referring to one's best clothes. The bib in question is not that used to keep babies clean during mealtimes, but refers to the top section of an apron which has the same name. A tucker was a frill of lace or muslin which women wore over their dresses in the seventeenth and eighteenth centuries to cover their necks and shoulders. To be in one's 'best bib and tucker', came to mean to be in one's finery, irrespective of the actual garments involved.

Best thing since sliced bread

The automation of modern baking which produces millions of identical loaves of bread was regarded as a major advance in food production by both producers and consumers. The US armed forces have been credited with coining 'the best thing since sliced bread' as a phrase of universal approval, which became widely used in the second half of the twentieth century.

Between the devil and the deep blue sea

Any impossible predicament can be described thus, but in naval parlance 'between the devil and the deep blue sea' had a particular meaning. The 'devil' referred to was a particularly inaccessible part of the ship's hull, either a seam at water-level, or a board attached to the hull to support the heavy guns run out above. In both cases reaching the 'devil' may have been hazardous, but it was unquestionably better than being lost in the 'deep blue sea'. Reference to the seam in the hull that required regular sealing to keep it watertight occurs in the expression 'the devil to pay and no pitch hot', which is the precursor to trouble arising from a recent event.

Betwixt wind and water

To a sailor the point on a ship's hull that is 'betwixt wind and water' is the point about the waterline that is sometimes below water, sometimes above it, depending on the weather and sea conditions. To be holed 'betwixt wind and water' is to be placed in grave danger of sinking. Hence the wider use of the expression to describe a situation of grave peril.

Beware Greeks bearing gifts

As a warning against being deceived, this recalls the story of the Trojan horse which led to the downfall of the ancient city of Troy. After ten years of fighting, the besieging Greek army constructed a large wooden horse, filled it with armed men and then withdrew as if they were returning home. The Trojans were persuaded to drag the horse inside the city, having been tricked by a captive left behind by the Greeks, into believing that it was an offering to the goddess Athene which would render Troy impregnable. Once the horse was inside the city walls, the same wily captive released the warriors hidden in it, who overpowered the guards and opened the city gates to the main Greek force which had returned under cover of darkness.

Beyond the pale

A 'pale' is a pointed stake used in a fence and by extension came to refer to the fence itself. In this way its meaning broadened to encompass the territory that lay within the boundary. This applied particularly to those areas of Ireland that were effectively under the control of the English crown during the Middle Ages. These shrank over the centuries and as they did so the areas 'beyond the pale' were regarded as returning to a wild and barbarous state. This meaning has survived as a description of someone's conduct that is outside the norms of civilized behaviour.

Biting the bullet

In the days before anaesthetics were available on the battlefield, the wounded had to be treated without painkillers. To brace themselves against the agony of their operations, patients were told to bite on the soft lead of a bullet, which would absorb the pressure of their bite without breaking their teeth. The expression has entered the language to describe preparing oneself for something unpleasant or painful.

Black sheep

Black sheep were once regarded as less valuable than white sheep. To the superstitious in bygone days they were seen to be carrying the mark of the devil. From this developed the idea of the 'black sheep' as being a disgrace to his or her family or close community.

Bob's your uncle

As an expression of reassurance that things will turn out to your benefit, 'Bob's your uncle' owes its origins to a real life 'Bob', the Conservative Prime Minister Lord Salisbury, whose first name was Robert. During his administration in the late 1880s, his nephew A. J. Balfour was rapidly promoted through the cabinet until he was made Secretary of State for Ireland. Few could deny that Uncle Bob had served his nephew well.

Boiled shirt

The stiff-fronted shirt worn by men in the evenings was commonly known as a 'boiled shirt' because of the starching process. It was also the name given to someone who was smug, dull-minded or priggish.

Born in the purple

According to ancient custom Byzantine emperors ensured that their successors were born in a special room decorated in the imperial purple that signified their royal status. Since those times 'born in the purple' has come to be a metaphor for anyone born into a noble family.

Born with a silver spoon in your mouth

The spoon alluded to is an Apostle's Spoon, a traditional christening present from a godparent. The expression suggests, however, that a child born into a wealthy family would have no need to wait for such a gift for his first taste of luxury. A complete set of Apostle's Spoons was, nonetheless, a generous gift. There are twelve, each with a different apostle at the top of the handle, and sometimes even an additional Master Spoon and Lady Spoon would be included.

Box and cox

Box and Cox was the title of a nineteenth-century farce which tells the story of two men, Box and Cox, who are let the same room by their deceitful landlady. One occupant works all day,

the other works all night and each makes use of the room wholly unaware of the other. From their predicament comes the expression to 'box and cox', meaning to alternate two or more situations simultaneously, frequently in a precarious manner.

Breaking your duck

Cricket is another game which has provided English with a number of enduring expressions, of which 'breaking your duck' is one. Players going in to bat start their innings with a score of nought. If they are dismissed before scoring any runs, they are 'out for a duck'. The phrase was originally 'out for a duck's egg', which makes the sense a little clearer, because of the resemblance of '0' to a duck's egg. However, 'duck's egg' became abbreviated to 'duck' and the expression has passed into the language of cricket. Some score-boards even have a symbol of a duck in profile, which is hung in place after a cricketer is dismissed after leaving the wicket with a score of nought.

However, scoring their first runs 'breaks their duck' and, from the cricket pitch, 'breaking your duck' has been put to use in any number of situations in which an individual starts to make progress by achieving the first, recognized goal or objective.

Broaching your claret

In the boxing ring 'claret' was adopted as a word for 'blood' because of its dark red colour. In order to draw claret (or any other liquid) from a barrel, the barrel has to be 'broached' with a tap. So in boxing 'broaching your claret' came to mean 'giving you a bloody nose'.

Burning the candle at both ends

This is said of someone who exhausts his energies by getting up early and staying up late or is wantonly extravagant. While it is not possible to light modern candles at both ends, the expression dates from the time when it was. Tallow candles, the common light of the common man, were made from animal fat and often had rush wicks protruding from either end. Such candles were held in a pincer-like stand or bracket that allowed either end of the candle to be lit. To light both ends simultaneously was considered to be extravagant in the extreme and someone who did so would be accused of being 'a candle-waster'.

Burying the hatchet

The hatchet was a key weapon of war among North American Indians. When conflicts had been settled, smoking the peace pipe was a signal that all weapons should be buried, so that all ideas of hostility would be hidden from sight. 'Burying the hatchet' today means letting bygones be bygones.

By a long chalk

It was once customary for many games to be scored by making chalk marks on a slate or other convenient surface. A long line of chalk marks indicated a clear winner and 'by a long chalk' acquired the meaning 'thoroughly', as in an expression like 'He beat me by a long chalk'. The phrase is used almost as much in a negative context, in which 'not by a long chalk' is an equally emphatic statement that something or someone will fail in a particular undertaking.

By hook or by crook

In medieval times tenants were granted the right by their lord of the manor to gather firewood 'by hook or by crook'; that is to say by using a shepherd's crook and a billhook. This was a legal entitlement of great value at a time when firewood was the sole means of providing heat with which to cook and warm the home. However, it also imposed restrictions on tenants, since it limited them to taking only wood that could be reached by the shepherd's crook and cut with the billhook; in other words, branches that could be reached down and cut from the ground.

The original meaning, of course, implied that taking wood 'by hook or by crook' was a lawful activity. In its modern usage, though, the implication is that anything undertaken 'by hook or by crook' is done either rightfully or wrongly in order to achieve its objective.

Called to the bar

The 'bar', which refers collectively to all professional barristers, takes its name from the Inns of Court. There fully-qualified barristers, or benchers, are separated from the students sitting in the main body of the hall by a partition: the 'bar'. When students have qualified as barristers, they are 'called to the bar' to be admitted as benchers.

Carpet knight

In the sixteenth century, when this expression first appears, it was used to describe a soldier who preferred his engagements to be in a lady's boudoir rather than on a battlefield. In the nineteenth century the name was applied contemptuously to any soldier who stayed at home. It is suggested that it stems from the days when a man was knighted on the carpet before the throne instead of, as was more common, on the battlefield.

Cast not a clout till May is out

Late April and early May can often be beset by the last blast of winter, when a cold wind sends temperatures falling. Since this frequently coincides with the flowering of the blackthorn, which turns the hedgerows white with blossom, the cold snap is known as a 'blackthorn winter'.

The warning, 'Cast not a clout till May is out', cautions against shedding winter clothing too early in the year.

Catch not a falling knife nor a falling friend

This rather uncharitable Victorian expression suggests that in either circumstance you risk being hurt. The inference is that to side with failure is somehow to bring disaster upon oneself.

Cat's pyjamas

The origin of this delightful expression is unknown but it is thought to have come to England from America. It is a variation of the 'cat's whiskers' or the 'bee's knees' and is used to say that something is excellent or worthy of praise. Real pyjamas, those not worn by cats, were brought back to England by travellers from India at the end of the eighteenth century. *Pajama*, in Hindi, is the name for the loose, baggy trousers worn as daywear by Muslims. The Hindi word comes from the Persian, *pa* meaning leg, and *jama* meaning garment. Either for climatic reasons or out of a sense of propriety, the English added a matching jacket, but kept the original name. Eventually 'pyjamas' took over from nightshirts as the most popular sleeping attire for men; and in the latter half of the twentieth century women also adopted the fashion.

Cherry picking

Since cherries have traditionally been picked by hand, there has always been an element of selection in choosing the ripest and most succulent fruit. From the country orchard, the expression has passed into modern business life, where 'cherry picking' has become widely used. Following the acquisition of one business interest by another, the dominant partner may be accused of cherry picking, if it selects the most profitable sectors of the business and concentrates on maximising returns from them at the expense of others which perform less well.

Chewing the cud

Among human beings, 'chewing the cud' describes a reflective state of mind in which people think deeply about something, especially the past.

The saying is a figurative borrowing, of course, referring to the digestive process of animals such as cattle, which are able to regurgitate food in order to chew it in their mouths again. Cattle in particular have a ruminative look about them while they chew the cud: the adjective 'ruminative' deriving from the noun 'ruminant', the name given to animals which chew the cud. Both English words stem from the Latin verb *ruminare*, which means 'to chew over again'.

Chock-a-block

When something is 'chock-a-block' it is filled right up with no space left. In naval terminology it describes the situation when two blocks used in a tackle are pulled together so that neither of them can be moved any further. In this context 'chock' means 'close up to' and when one block is so close to another that it cannot move it is 'chock-a-block'.

Clew up

On a sailing ship a 'clew' was the corner of the sail to which ropes were attached. When a sail was 'clewed up' the corners were hauled up to the yard from which it was suspended, so that the sail could be furled. From this has grown the meaning of 'clew up' – to finish something completely, to be ready to do something with everything fully prepared.

Climbing on the bandwagon

In days gone by it was common in the USA for a band to be paraded on a wagon through the streets to advertise political meetings or other public gatherings. In the case of meetings held prior to elections, local dignitaries showed their support for candidates by climbing onto their particular wagons. Since then 'climbing on the bandwagon' has been taken as a display of support for a popular movement in the hope of personal profit or advantage.

Close as a Kentish oyster

For hundreds of years Kent has been renowned for the quality of its oysters. All oysters need to be tightly closed to ensure that they are good to eat, and oysters from Kent were regarded as being shut tighter than most. So anything described as being 'close as a Kentish oyster' was similarly shut fast, from which developed its wider meaning of 'absolutely secret'

Cock crow at bedtime

Many birds announce the arrival of rain and the farmyard cock is one of the most noticeable. The sound of a cock's crowing is usually associated with dawn; however, if it crows in the evening, it foretells the onset of rain:

> If the cocks crow when they go to bed,
> They'll sure to come down with a watery head.

In other words it will rain the following morning.

Cocking a snook

A 'snook' is a derisive gesture made by placing the thumb on the nose and spreading the fingers. 'Cocking a snook' lends to this an air of swaggering defiance, alluding to the stance of fighting cocks. The adjective 'cocky' follows a similar meaning.

Coming up to scratch

'Coming up to scratch' is a term from both athletics and boxing. Until the comparatively recent introduction of starting blocks and running tracks with special surfaces, competitors for a running race used to line up along a line scratched in the ground. A similar line was used in early boxing matches as well, when both contestants had to begin each round standing with one foot touching a line scratched on the ground. If either of them failed 'to come up scratch' at the start of a round, he lost the fight. Since those times, 'coming up to scratch' has been used in the sense of 'achieving a recognized standard'. Failing to 'come up to scratch' means failing to live up to expectations.

Cook your goose

The first time this expression appeared in print was around 1850 and it is thought to have been a line in a popular play in which one of the characters decides that to save his own 'bacon' he must, in turn, cook another's goose. It means to bring about the ruin or downfall of another – or oneself, in the case of cooking one's own goose. There is no reliable evidence to explain why a goose is the chosen bird or, indeed, why cooking it should be so significant. It may possibly refer to a goose, being fattened for the table where it is due to take pride of place on a special occasion, that is eaten prematurely, leaving nothing for the event for which it is has been designated.

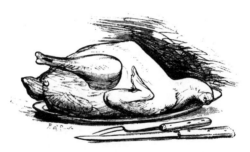

Cupboard love

A show of love based on self-interest or the prospect of gain is called 'cupboard love'. It is thought to stem from the childish practice of lavishing affection on any indulgent person who provides tasty morsels or treats from the store. In the early nineteenth century it was commonly understood that 'cupboard love is seldom true'. As for cupboards – a cupboard was originally just what it says it was – an open board or plank on which to store cups and plates. By 1530 it had taken on the meaning of being 'a closet or cabinet with shelves for keeping cups, dishes, provisions etc' and had moved out of the kitchen. Henry VIII had a cupboard of twelve shelves for displaying his gold ware, the number of shelves one could display being determined by one's status. It is noted in *The Life of Cardinal Wolsey*, by George Cavendish, that the proud man boasted a 'Cup Borde . . . six desks [shelves] high'. Dukes, on the other hand, were permitted only four or five, lesser noblemen three, and the mere gentleman only one.

Curate's egg

A cartoon in *Punch* magazine dating from 1895 gave rise to the expression 'good in parts, like the curate's egg'. In the cartoon a nervous young curate, seated at his bishop's breakfast table, is addressed by his lordship who says, 'I'm afraid you've got a bad egg, Mr Jones!' The curate, desperate not to offend, replies, 'Oh no, my Lord, I assure you! Parts of it are excellent!' From this, 'good in parts, like the curate's egg' has come to describe something 'patchy' and of uneven quality.

Curtain lecture

One has to envisage a fully draped four-poster to understand why this is the term used to describe a private reproof of a husband by his wife once they are alone and the curtains on the bed are drawn. Dryden was so disdainful of the habit he wrote:

> Besides what endless brawls by wives are bred,
> The curtain lecture makes a mournful bed.

In 1886 such scoldings also became known as Caudle Lectures, from a series published in *Punch* in which a character, Mr Caudle, suffered the nagging of his wife once they had retired to bed.

Cut the mustard

When someone is said to have 'cut the mustard' it means they have done a thing well, particularly when it was suspected beforehand that they might not. As well as being a popular condiment, mustard became a slang term for 'the best'. There is one school of thought that favours the idea that the 'cutting' relates to the harvesting of a notoriously difficult plant to glean, thereby implying that only the best can undertake the task. Another idea suggests that the term comes from the practice of adding vinegar to 'cut' or reduce the bitterness of the mustard seeds when creating the familiar paste. (The simile, 'as keen as mustard' alludes to the sharpness of the condiment.) Yet another notion is that the term is a confusion of the military expression 'cut the muster' which means well turned-out both in appearance and punctuality. Whatever its origin, it is patently clear that *not* to 'cut the mustard' signifies a total failure to achieve the required standard.

Dark horse

In the world of horse-racing, a 'dark horse' is a runner, entered for a race, about which there is little hard information but which seems to have the potential to run well and maybe win.

Transferred to people, 'dark horse' is applied to someone whose abilities and likely course of action are unknown.

Daylight robbery

This is a term that is applied to an extortionate or excessive charge for something. The allusion is that the action is overtly carried out without any attempt to disguise or conceal it. There is a school of thought, however, that favours the explanation that the expression came about from the much-hated Window Tax that was first introduced in 1695 and lasted, in various revised forms, until it was finally abolished in 1851. During this period many homeowners blocked up windows to reduce their liability, and no doubt considered the Crown guilty of 'daylight robbery'. As enchanting an idea as this is, unfortunately it remains unsubstantiated. As an aside, there are still many people who confuse the windows blocked up to avoid payment of Window Tax with the false windows that were often incorporated into homes to maintain the exterior symmetry and proportions.

Dead as a doornail

The 'doornail' in question is the large-headed stud that is hit by the doorknocker. The assumption is that anything that takes such a hard and constant pounding must, indeed, be totally lifeless. Variations on the saying included 'dead as a herring', 'dead as Julius Caesar', and 'dead as a tent-peg' but the 'doornail' has survived them all.

Dine with Duke Humphrey

Far from being entertained to a lavish meal, 'to dine with Duke Humphrey' meant going without dinner altogether. Humphrey, the Duke of Gloucester, was the youngest son of Henry IV and renowned for his generosity and hospitality. It was rumoured when he died that a monument would be erected to him in St Paul's. In reality it never was, but another tomb was popularly supposed to be his, and people seeking sanctuary within the church's precinct and consequently with no dinner to go to, would say that they were to 'dine with Duke Humphrey' that night. The expression was well understood in its day, as was a similar but later one, to 'sup with Sir Thomas Gresham'. Gresham was the merchant financier who founded and built the Royal Exchange, which, business apart, became a favourite haunt for loungers. Such habits were even later encapsulated in Robert Hayman's 1628 *Quodlibets*, which includes *Epigram on a Loafer*:

> Though little coin thy purseless pocket line,
> Yet with great company thou art taken up;
> For often with Duke Humphrey thou dost dine,
> And often with Sir Thomas Gresham sup.

Both expressions remained in common use until the early nineteenth century.

Dining with the cross-legged knights

To 'dine with the cross-legged knights' is to go without any dinner at all. The 'cross-legged knights' referred to were the stone effigies of Templar knights in their old Temple Church in

London, which later became a meeting place for lawyers and their clients. This was also the haunt of layabouts who frequented the Temple on the off-chance of being hired as witnesses.

Don't count your chickens before they are hatched

The origin of this well-known proverb lies in one of Aesop's fables which tells the tale of a dairy maid so preoccupied with the eggs she was going to buy with the proceeds from the sale of her milk, that she lost concentration and allowed the pail to fall over, losing all her milk in the process.

From this cautionary tale, the saying 'Don't count your chickens before they are hatched' has become a well-established warning not to make, or act on, an assumption which turns out to be wrong, even if the prospects appear to be favourable.

Don't look a gift horse in the mouth

This saying has a similar meaning to 'Straight from the horse's mouth' and both allude to the common practice of examining a horse's front teeth to establish its age.

'Don't look a gift horse in the mouth' warns the recipient of a present against enquiring too closely into its intrinsic value. The advice at the root of the expression is, be happy to have received the gift and leave it at that.

Drawing a bow at a venture

Archery, and military archery in particular, has furnished English with a number of expressions that have long outlived the use of the longbow in warfare. 'Drawing a bow at a venture' is one of these turns of phrase, now meaning to attack without taking proper aim and, by analogy, to make a chance remark that coincidentally goes to the truth of a matter.

Drawing blank

Those who 'draw blank' fail in what they are trying to achieve. The allusion is to the hunting field where sportsmen would 'draw' a covert to flush out game that might be hiding there. If no game emerged, the draw was a 'blank' and the hunt was obliged to move to another likely location.

Dressed up to the nines

There are two explanations for why someone who is over-dressed for an occasion or dressed in a fussy manner should be said to be 'dressed up to the nines'. The first is based on 'nines' being a corruption of the Old English word for eyes, *eyne*. Someone dressed up to his or her eyes would be over-dressed indeed. The other theory is that as ten is the number associated with perfection, nine is just one step short and therefore excellent.

Drinking a toast

An old custom demanded that toast should be put into tankards of beer to improve their flavour. Strange as this appears, it is no more bizarre than the story in a very early edition of the *Tatler*, which introduced the practice of drinking 'toasts' as a compliment to individuals or institutions. The story goes that during the reign of Charles II, a renowned beauty was in the Cross Bath at Bath, when one of her admirers took a glass of the water in which she was standing and drank her health to all present. This prompted another gentleman, who had been indulging in stronger drink than water, to exclaim that he would jump in the water, for, 'though he liked not the liquor, he would have the toast', in other words the lady herself. Thereafter, compliments expressed publicly and accompanied by a drink became known as 'toasts'.

"YOU'LL NEVER MISS THE WATER"

Dyed in the wool

'Dyed in the wool' dates from the time when the wool trade and associated cloth industry in England was well established and serving a growing market at home and on the Continent.

Cloth that was made from wool which had been dyed before weaving, in other words dyed in the wool, kept its colour for much longer than cloth that had been dyed after weaving.

From this practical example of durability and reliability stemmed the wider use of the phrase which came to mean 'thorough-going' and 'one hundred per cent' – the antithesis of short-lived and superficial.

Eating Dunmow bacon

Old tradition in Dunmow in Essex held that any person who could honestly swear (and prove) that for the previous twelve months and a day he or she had never had a row with their spouse and never wished themselves unmarried, could claim a gammon of bacon, known as a flitch. The tradition of the Dunmow Flitch dates from the twelfth century and 'eating Dunmow bacon' is a well-established term for a happily married life.

Eating humble pie

The food served at a medieval hunting feast established a marked social distinction between diners. The lord, his family and guests were served venison at high table. Further down the table, those of lesser standing, the huntsmen and retainers, fed on a pie made of the deer's heart, liver and entrails, or 'umbles'. 'Humble pie' is a pun on 'umble pie' and those presented with it are required, metaphorically, to eat inferior food in an inferior position.

Anyone made to 'eat humble pie' is forced to come down from a lofty position they have wrongly assumed, in order to defer to others; frequently those they had previously looked down on.

Eavesdropper

If guttering had been invented in the fifth century, the name for someone who listens secretly to other people's private conversations might be completely different. As it was, under Saxon law, homeowners were obliged to leave a space around their property for the water that ran off the eaves. Such a space was known as an *yfes drype*, eaves-drip or eaves-drop. Anyone who placed himself inside that space to hear what was going on in the house, consequently became known as an 'eavesdropper'.

Eggs on the spit

The full expression is 'I have eggs on the spit' and it means that you are very busy indeed and have no time for other matters. The reference is to an old, time-consuming recipe and the 'spit' is a toasting fork, rather than the conventional spit we think of for roasting meat. To roast an egg is not as impossible as it sounds. First you boil your egg, peel it and remove the yolk. That you mix with a variety of spices and then replace the mixture into the egg, before carefully threading the stuffed egg onto a toasting fork and holding it over the fire. Such a delicate concoction required close attention or the dish would be ruined.

Elbow grease

The perspiration caused by hard manual labour was known, in the seventeenth century, in a derisory way, as 'elbow grease'. In time, the term was applied to the energy needed to undertake such tasks as might generate the sweat in the first place. Whether knowingly or unknowingly, that change echoed the thinking of the early Greeks, who considered sweat to be the essence of strength and vigour. The reasoning was that if a man exerted himself to the extent that he sweated, he was sapped of energy and drained. Therefore, the fluid itself must be an essential part of physical power. There are tales of soldiers spreading the sweat of their horses onto their own bodies to improve their strength; and it was not unheard of for men to

drink the sweat of famous warriors in the conviction that it contained courage. When we wish someone 'all power to your elbow', if they are undertaking a seemingly difficult task, we may not know it, but we are harking back to the earliest Greek physiology. The potency of 'elbow grease', still considered to be 'the best furniture oil', remains undiminished.

Every tub must stand on its own bottom

This rather delightful Elizabethan expression means that there are some things you have to do for yourself and that cannot be done by others. The reference is to the solid tubs that were used for a variety of domestic chores, particularly in the laundry.

Facing the music

The military origin of this expression is similar to that of 'drummed out', referring to the formal, humiliating dismissal of a soldier from his regiment. The ceremony involved the beating of drums, a public reading of the culprit's crime and the stripping of insignia from his uniform. Thus, 'facing the music' became associated with bearing punishment in general.

Feather in your cap

To earn a 'feather in one's cap' is to have done something that earns you praise or acclaim. Far from being rooted in sartorial fashion, the expression is believed to come from the custom of the ancient Lycians, later Asian cultures and North American tribes, who added a feather to their headwear for each enemy they killed.

February fill dyke, black or white

One way or another February feels a wet month, even if the rainfall is low. Cold weather and a weak sun mean that dampness lingers. Whether rain or snow falls, in February ditches invariably fill with water, giving rise to the saying.

Feeling your oats

Common belief maintains that horses are friskier and more energetic after they have eaten oats. Based on this assumption, the saying has been applied over the years to people as well, so that anyone described as 'feeling their oats' can be taken to be behaving in a lively, self-important way, indicative of the fact that they feel well pleased with themself.

Fine kettle of fish

A 'fine kettle of fish' (sometimes a 'pretty kettle of fish') means a 'muddle', or a 'messy business' and refers to the riverside picnic of the same name which forms a part of the traditional salmon fishing season in parts of Scotland. In this 'kettle of fish', freshly caught salmon are immediately put into a pot of boiling water right on the river bank. As soon as the fish are cooked, they are eaten by hand. Delicious as the result may be, the process is understandably messy, which accounts for its association with an unfortunate predicament.

Fitting to a "T"

The allusion here is to a draughtsman's T-square, the ruler with a cross-piece at one end set precisely at right angles, which makes it possible to make accurate drawings, and draw parallel lines and right angles. In this expression anything that 'fits to a T', fits exactly.

Flash in the pan

A 'flash in the pan' is an enterprise that begins brightly but soon fails after a very brief success. The allusion is to flintlock guns in which a small measure of gunpowder, ignited in the lockpan, detonated the main charge. It was not uncommon for the powder in the lockpan to fail to set off the charge in the breech. When this happened the 'flash in the pan' failed to carry out its objective.

Flavour of the month

Competition in the ice-cream business in America led to ice-cream parlours across the country promoting their business by featuring a special 'flavour of the month', often at a reduced price to attract custom. By the 1980s the phrase had come to describe anything or anyone temporarily in vogue.

Flowers out of season

The whole saying goes: 'Flowers out of season, trouble without reason'.

Any interruption to the orderly rhythm of nature has always been taken as a portent of uncertain times ahead and the blooming of flowers out of season was once seen by many country dwellers as foretelling death or disaster.

From pillar to post

The ancient game of 'real tennis' gave rise to this expression, which means moving from one thing to another without any clear objective or direction. The analogy is to the flight of a tennis ball in a 'real tennis' court. Unlike lawn tennis, the ball in this game can strike the walls as well as the floor (as does the ball in a game of squash). However, the walls of a 'real tennis' court contain a number of protrusions which can make the ball fly off

in unexpected directions. These resembled 'pillars' and 'posts' in the medieval 'courts' where the game was first played and are now incorporated into the design of all 'real tennis' courts.

Full of beans

At first 'full of beans' was an expression used to describe a horse that was in prime condition and full of energy. The contribution made by beans to the animal's excellent state of health is unclear; as a source of nourishment, beans may have been equated with energy and vitality.

Come the nineteenth century humans too were benefiting, metaphorically, from the energy-enhancing influence of beans. So anyone deemed to be in 'high spirits' and generally on 'good form' could aptly be described as being 'full of beans' too.

Getting down to brass tacks

In old-fashioned drapers' shops it was common for cloth to be measured against the shiny heads of brass tacks, driven into the counter at even distances apart. 'Getting down to brass tacks' recalls this process of determining precisely what was required.

Getting your ducks in a row

The impression conveyed in this popular American expression is one of order and organization. The 'ducks' referred to are actually skittles, rather than farmyard fowls, and 'getting your ducks in a row' originally meant setting up your skittles, before it was borrowed to be used in the wider sense of 'having your affairs completed and in order'.

Get your shirt out

This expression means to become angry or quarrelsome. It is thought that it alludes to the idea of a man pulling his shirt from his trousers in readiness to strip for a fight. We still use a variation of the phrase in modern speech, when we refer to someone as being 'shirty' or bad-tempered.

Give someone the cold shoulder

Used figuratively, this means to be reserved and unwelcoming. The common view is that it comes from the practice of the host who, rather than offering a sumptuous meal, serves cold shoulder of mutton for dinner (a meal usually reserved only for servants and the like) as a way of telling an unwanted guest that he has outstayed his welcome. Appealing as this explanation is, the more plausible is that it was a Scottish expression of unknown origin popularized by Walter Scott's use of it in his novel *The Antiquary*, in 1816: 'The Countess's dislike didna gang farther at first than just showing the cauld shouther'; the 'cauld shouther' expressing the idea of a physical dismissive movement rather than a reference to cold meat. What is certain, is that the expression was established in common parlance by the mid-nineteenth century.

Going off at half-cock

The hunting field can be hazardous, and in the early days of firearms, it was not the game alone that faced danger from the guns. Firing an old-fashioned flintlock gun involved releasing a spring-loaded hammer called a 'cock'. Freed by the action of the trigger, this struck a piece of flint against a steel plate, sending sparks into the small charge of powder in the lockpan, which in turn detonated the main charge in the breech of the gun. When the gun was fully cocked, it could only be discharged by pulling the trigger. At 'half-cock', however, it was liable to go off unexpectedly, often before there had been time to take aim, with the result that the shot was frequently wasted.

That is why anything described as 'going off at half-cock' can be taken as premature, ill-prepared and unlikely to succeed.

Going to pot

This expression, meaning to be ruined or destroyed, does little to flatter culinary art. It refers to meat or vegetables being chopped up into small enough pieces to be thrown into the ubiquitous cooking pot, the implication being that the value of it is lost forever. It is thought to be a shorter version of the expression 'go to the pot' which was known to be in use in the mid-sixteenth century.

Going wool-gathering

During the Middle Ages villagers who were thought to be incapable of other work were set to gather wool torn from sheep by bushes and brambles. Quite apart from the mental state of the wool-gatherers, this necessitated wandering about the fields and hedgerows apparently aimlessly. In time 'going wool-gathering' became a term used of anyone who showed signs of day-dreaming or absent-mindedness.

Gone for a Burton

'Gone for a Burton' was another euphemism for 'missing, presumed dead' which became popular during the Second World War. No definitive explanation of its origin has been arrived at, but once again the RAF appears to have had a hand in its evolution. From the 1880s 'Burton-on-Trent' (often abbreviated to 'Burton') was rhyming slang for 'rent'. If the wartime connection lies here, it might allude to the missing serviceman paying his due, or possibly going missing to avoid paying rent. More likely is the brewing association with Burton-on-Trent which has been an important producer of beer for several hundred years. Aircrew shot down in the sea were said to have come down in 'the drink', thereby going for a beer or 'going for a Burton'. One other likely explanation links the expression with the British firm of men's tailors and outfitters called Burton. Above their headquarters in Blackpool, RAF signal operators were trained in Morse code and radio operation; those who failed their final assessment were said to have 'gone for a Burton'.

Go through with a fine-tooth comb

Anyone who has had to deal with a louse-infected head will appreciate how thorough and painstaking a search with a 'fine-tooth comb' really is. The expression refers, of course, to the use of a nit comb, which has exceptionally thin and closely-set teeth.

PRESCRIPTIONS

Grasping the nettle

Pulling nettles can be an uncomfortable experience, as anyone who has weeded a garden over-run with nettles will tell you. However, nettles are less likely to sting a bare hand if they are held tightly rather than tentatively. Hence the countryman's wise advice to grasp nettles tightly, to avoid being stung by them, as the poet Aaron Hill commented in the first half of the eighteenth century:

> Tender-handed stroke a nettle
> And it stings you for your pains;
> Grasp it like a man of mettle,
> And it soft as silk remains.

This is carried into the metaphorical sense of the saying when it is used as an encouragement to face difficulties firmly and to tackle situations boldly.

Hair of the dog

An old folk remedy for healing a wound caused by a dog bite, was to place on the wound a burnt hair from the dog which had given the bite. Unlikely as it may seem, this was believed to be the best cure for dog bites.

From this has come the metaphorical use of the term 'hair of the dog' to describe an old cure for a hangover, which consists of drinking the following morning a little of the same beverage that had brought on the hangover in the first place. So, 'hair of the dog' is often the rueful comment made by the sufferer of a hangover at the first taste of drink the following day.

Handle with kid gloves

The leather from the hide of young goats was considered the finest, and was one of the most expensive leathers to be used in the glove industry. Their delicacy and value meant that kid-leather gloves were kept to be worn when there was no danger of having to undertake any manual task. Therefore, anything or anyone that is given the 'kid-glove' treatment is handled with extreme tact and gentleness.

Having no truck with

The old French word *troquer*, meaning 'to barter' is a pointer towards the background of this phrase. To 'have no truck with' someone is to avoid any dealings with them, especially business dealings. At one time workers were paid all or part of their wages in accordance with the truck system, whereby they were paid in goods, or tokens that could be exchanged for goods, controlled by their employers. A series of government measures abolished the system during the nineteenth century by which time it had become totally discredited. 'Having no truck' in these circumstances meant a refusal to accept payment by the truck system.

He sups ill who eats all at dinner

This is a Victorian homily against being profligate with your means when you are young. The inference was that if you spent everything in your youth, you faced the prospect of destitution in old age. (A shorter but less elegant version of the expression is: 'Shoed in the cradle, barefoot in the stubble'.)

Hiding your light under a bushel

In times gone by grain and other dry goods were measured in a wooden or earthenware container, holding, and therefore known as, a 'bushel'.

Self-evidently, anything placed under the upturned bushel would be hidden from sight. So those who were modest and self-effacing about their abilities were described as hiding their light 'under a bushel', where their talents remained hidden from the sight of others.

Hit the sack

For many people the luxury of a proper bed was beyond their means. In such instances makeshift mattresses would be made by stuffing sacks with straw. 'To hit the sack', therefore, is merely to go to bed. The expression has lasted long after such rudimentary beds were commonplace.

Hobson's choice

In reality 'Hobson's choice' amounts to having no choice at all. The phrase is said to take its name from a Cambridge horse-keeper by the name of Thomas Hobson, who insisted on only releasing his horses for use in the order stipulated by him. Those wishing to hire horses from him either accepted Hobson's choice or went without a horse.

Hoist with his own petard

A 'petard' was a siege weapon made of iron and filled with gunpowder which was used in medieval warfare to blow a breach in a wall or fortified gate. Placing and detonating 'petards' was a hazardous process, not only from the attack by defending troops, but also from the explosive device itself. Engineers who fired petards risked being killed by their premature explosion and one who perished in this way was 'hoist with his own petard'. The

phrase has been used figuratively since then with reference to anyone who is caught in his own trap, or caught out by his own subterfuge.

I don't care a fig for you

The fig was not a feature of the English rural diet, or its husbandry, in days gone by.

So it presents an apparent problem in this popular turn of phrase. That is until we realize that the 'fig' referred to is not the tasty fruit of the fig tree, but the 'figo' or 'fico' (also known as the 'Spanish fig'). This was a common gesture of contempt, made with the thumb and fingers, which was well known in the England of Shakespeare's day. In *Henry V* Shakespeare offers this definition in the hot-headed exchange between Pistol and Fluellen:

Pistol:	Die and be damn'd! and figo for thy friendship!
Fluellen:	It's well.
Pistol:	The fig of Spain!

'I don't care a fig for you' and similar turns of phrase, such as 'I don't give a fig' carry the same unmistakable meaning as snapping one's fingers at someone while declaring 'I don't care that for you.'

If beards were all, then goats would preach

This is a more recent version of the older proverb 'An old goat is never the more revered for his beard'. Both carry the meaning that old age alone (identified by the reference to beards) is not a hallmark of wisdom and that true wisdom lies deeper than superficial appearances.

If the cap fits, wear it

This expression is still very common today and means that if a remark or description is applicable, then you should apply it to yourself. However, in a more literal sense, it might have been wise to check first, as there was a law that decreed just what headwear could be worn by people of different ranks. In the 1568 Bailiff's Accounts for Leominster, in Herefordshire, for example, there is an entry recording that several persons were fined for wearing caps beyond their station in life.

If you can't stand the heat, get out of the kitchen

Plain-speaking Harry S. Truman, the thirty-third president of the United States who held office from 1945 until 1953, coined a number of memorable down-to-earth maxims, of which this became one of the most widely used. As he wrote in *Mr Citizen*, published in 1960, 'I used to have a saying that applies here, and I note that some people have picked it up: "If you can't stand the heat, get out of the kitchen".' The allusion to slaving over a hot stove, while under pressure to prepare a meal, is well applied to other situations in the sense of 'if you can't take the strain, don't get involved'.

In meal or in malt

Millers were frequently regarded with suspicion by their neighbours. Many people were convinced that the miller regularly took more than his fair share of the harvest as it passed through his hands.

This underlying doubt about a miller's conduct and honesty, gave rise to the saying 'in meal or in malt': both of which were end products of the grain milled by the miller.

Since both meal and malt had the potential to produce a profit, and since the miller was entitled to a share of the proceeds as his payment, he would benefit whatever the milled grain was used for.

'In meal or in malt' then is a figurative rendering of 'in one way or the other', or 'directly or indirectly'.

In the morning sow thy seed

The movement of the sun is said to have an effect on plant growth. Where circumstances allowed, farmers tried to sow corn and similar crops in the morning, while the sun was still rising towards noon. Root crops, potatoes and the like, which grow below ground, were reckoned to prefer afternoon sowing, so that they could 'sink down' with the sun.

The same distinction was drawn when grass was mown: cutting grass in the morning was believed to promote growth, whereas cutting grass in the afternoon was supposed to have the opposite effect.

It won't wash

For the origin of this expression, one must go back to the days when printed calico was in vogue. If you were wealthy you could afford fabric woven with integral patterns, but if not an alternative was printed calico. The problem was that printed calico could not withstand any form of laundering for fear the pattern would be washed off. To say something 'wouldn't wash', therefore was to imply that it was of little permanent value.

Nowadays, the expression implies more that something 'will not hold water' and is said of an excuse or explanation that is obviously far-fetched or unbelievable. As an aside, the inferiority of the material that gave rise to 'it won't wash' is reflected in the name given to cheap, public dances: they were called 'Calico Balls'.

Join the household brigade

When the threat of war was on everyone's mind and the various regiments were actively recruiting new men, this expression took hold. It meant, quite simply, to get married.

Jumping over the broomstick

'Jumping over the broomstick' has become a euphemism for a marriage that takes place quite informally without significant preparation or ceremony.

It is a curious saying which owes its origin to the practice, observed among itinerant country groups especially, of establishing 'married status' through the happy couple's ceremonial jumping over a broomstick; or 'jumping over a besom' to quote an alternative form.

Keeping up with the Joneses

Anyone trying to maintain appearances or keep on the social level of their neighbours has been 'keeping up with the Joneses' since before the First World War. In 1913 a cartoon series began to be syndicated in newspapers throughout the USA based on the attempts by the artist, Arthur R. ('Pop') Momand, to keep up with his neighbours. It was he who invented the phrase.

Kicking the bucket

At the beginning of winter it was once common for households to slaughter the pig which they had been fattening through the year. Once killed, the pig's carcass was suspended from a wooden frame, known in the eastern parts of England as a 'bucket', from the French word *buquet* for a beam. Hanging by its heels, it was not uncommon for the carcass to undergo the occasional post-mortem spasm, which made it 'kick the bucket'. From this derived the euphemism for dying which we know today.

Killing the fatted calf

The parable of the prodigal son as told in St Luke's gospel gave rise to this expression meaning 'to celebrate' and 'to welcome with the best of everything'. In the parable Christ tells the story of two brothers, the elder of whom remains at home, working diligently, while his younger brother takes his share of his inheritance and leaves home to squander it. In time the younger brother sees the error of his ways and returns home in due humility to ask his father for forgiveness and to be allowed back, even in the capacity of a farm labourer. However, his father is so overjoyed to see him again that he offers him presents and arranges a welcoming feast which necessitates 'killing the fatted calf' kept for important celebrations. The elder brother resents the reception his brother has received until his father explains,

in the words of the gospel, 'Son, thou art ever with me, and all that I have is thine. It was meet that we should make merry, and be glad: for this thy brother was dead, and is alive again; and was lost, and is found.'

'Killing the goose which laid the golden egg

The need to balance supply with demand could be a crucial issue in country districts when winter supplies had to be eked out and stocks of seed preserved for the next year's sowing. It was Aesop who enshrined the fable of the goose who laid the golden eggs with proverbial wisdom, but the message it bore has resonated in rural societies ever since.

In Aesop's fable a countryman blessed with a goose which laid golden eggs, thought to make himself even richer by killing the goose, in order to grab all the golden eggs at once. This reckless act, of course, ended the supply of the very eggs he coveted.

Ever since that time, 'killing the goose that laid the golden eggs' has become a metaphor warning against sacrificing future reward and security for immediate gain.

Knocking the spots off

'Knocking the spots off' someone means to 'beat them soundly' and 'easily get the better of them'. The allusion is to demonstrating a high level of skill at shooting. In the late nineteenth century, skilled marksmen, with both pistols and rifles, used to display their expertise by shooting at playing cards,

with the aim of 'knocking out the spots' or pips. Only the best shots were able to do this and their success set them far above less accomplished ones.

Knowing how many beans make five

Anyone who knows 'how many beans make five' is no fool. More to the point, he or she is not to be put upon.

The reference is to a traditional catch: How many beans make five? The answer, self-evidently, is five. Then comes the supplementary question: But how many blue beans make five white beans? The correct answer is five – when they have been peeled.

Know which side your bread is buttered

For hundreds of years this term has been used to describe someone who is aware of where his best interests lie, even though butter was despised as a food by the upper and middle classes until the eighteenth century when it became popular as a spread for bread. (Prior to that butter was principally used as a medicine. It was made mainly in the spring and the summer and heavily salted to preserve it for future use. As a curious aside, butter made in May was considered particularly beneficial to children for the treatment of constipation and growing pains!)

Knuckling under

Today we reserve the word 'knuckle' to describe finger-joints, but in earlier times it had a wider meaning covering any bone that ended in a joint. In this context 'knuckling under' meant kneeling as a display of submission or admitting defeat. The phrase we use today carries the same meaning of giving in.

Land of milk and honey

The biblical origin of this expression has led to its figurative use in denoting the blessings of heaven. A 'land of milk and honey' is one of great fertility in which nourishing and plentiful food can be produced. The phrase comes from the Book of Exodus, where God tells Moses of the land to which he will lead the children of Israel from captivity in Egypt: 'And I am come down to deliver them out of the hand of the Egyptians, and to bring them up out of that land unto a good land and a large, unto a land flowing with milk and honey.'

Laugh up your sleeve

There was a time when sleeves were so long and loose that it was quite possible to cover one's face if one wanted to hide one's expression. Figuratively, however, the expression means to laugh to oneself, especially in a derisory or dismissive manner.

Leave some for the Duke of Rutland

For centuries children were encouraged to leave a little food on their plates, following the wisdom of the Bible, in which it states: 'Leave off first for manners' sake; and be not unsatiable, lest thou offend.' The family name of the Duke of Rutland was 'Manners', and thus his name became a substitute for the original noun.

Let every man soap his own beard

Over the centuries there have been many expressions centred on the call for everyone to look after his own affairs, and this is yet another. It implies that we must all be accountable for what we do and should not rely on others.

Letting the cat out of the bag

A secret is revealed if 'the cat is let out of the bag' and in the days when this originated that is precisely what happened. The cat would have been put in the bag by an unscrupulous market trader hoping to pass it off as a young sucking pig, similar to the one on open display at his stall. Unwitting buyers would pay for a pig in one of the sacks only to find later that they had bought a puppy or a cat instead. Those who had the good sense to check what they were buying would 'let the cat out of the bag' and reveal the trick that was being played on them.

Lick into shape

In the Middle Ages there was a widespread belief that bear cubs were born shapeless and had to be licked into the shape of bears by their mothers. Applied to human offspring, it describes the process of rearing children to behave in an appropriate way and generally it means making things presentable.

Life is just a bowl of cherries

The American musical *Scandals of 1931* included among its songs 'Life is just a bowl of cherries'. Written by Lew Brown, with music by Ray Henderson, this was popularized by Ethel Merman and helped establish the title as a proverbial expression that 'everything is wonderful'.

Little pitchers have wide ears

This was used as a warning that it was unwise to say anything in front of children that you did not wish repeated. Common kitchen vessels for centuries, pitchers were traditionally large earthenware pots with a lip and two large ear-shaped handles.

Loading the dice

'Loaded dice' are dice which have been illegally weighted, so that they fall with the required face up. Therefore 'loading the dice' is an act designed to gain advantage over an opponent. The term is used in expressions like 'loading the dice against' someone, which means prejudicing their chances of success.

Locking the stable door after the horse has bolted

Less of a problem than it might once have been, now that cars have replaced horses as the principal mode of transport for many in the countryside and beyond, this proverb is still very much in use.

Its image is graphic and its message stark: taking precautions against a mishap *after* it has happened is a complete waste of time and effort.

Mackerel sky won't last twenty-four hours dry

A mackerel sky, the layer of mottled cloud which resembles the colour and patina of a mackerel's skin is a well-known forerunner of rain, though usually a shower of rain rather than a heavy storm. Many sayings record this, for example: 'Mackerel sky – rain is nigh' and 'Mackerel sky, mackerel sky, never long wet, never long dry'.

Mad as a hatter

A mercury-based chemical used in the manufacture of felt hats was thought to be responsible for creating tremulous conditions such as St Vitus Dance in those who were exposed to them for a prolonged period. The nature of their trade made hatters susceptible, though the phrase owes much of its popularity to Lewis Carroll who popularized it in *Alice in Wonderland*.

Mad as a March hare

March is the month in which hares breed, a time of the year when they indulge in their elaborate and energetic courtship displays. Leaping and running about wildly, the hares appear to be behaving out of character, giving rise to the notion that they are in some way mad.

By association, any individual who behaves abnormally and somewhat recklessly might be termed as 'mad as a March hare' too.

Make hay while the sun shines

Although very few of us make hay today, we know the value of taking advantage of an opportunity; or striking while the iron is hot, to draw an analogy with the blacksmith's shop.

Before the days of mechanical cutting, tedding and baling, fine weather was essential to ensure a satisfactory crop of hay. Today a wet spell during haymaking can cause difficulties for even the best-equipped farmer.

Make no bones about it

Saying or doing something without delay regardless of the consequences is to 'make no bones about it'. As a process of coming straight to the point, it takes its origins from dice, which were once referred to as bones. There is an expression in French which describes sliding the dice, a process that has been taken as softening something down. This is the precise opposite of the English expression, which has no interest in manipulating the dice to curry favour. Plain speaking is the order of the day when we 'make no bones' about something.

Making bricks without straw

In the Book of Exodus the Egyptians command the Israelites to make bricks without straw, a process which is doomed to failure, for without straw the bricks will crumble and break. Thus any attempt to do something without proper materials and preparation will meet a similar fate.

Meet on the stairs and you won't meet in heaven

This is just one of the many superstitions surrounding the humble staircase and underlines the concerns people held about passing someone else on the stairs. Such a meeting was to be avoided at all costs and the onus was on the person at the top of the stairs to wait until the person going up or going down had reached his destination. If this was not possible, the two people

concerned needed to cross their fingers as they passed, in the hope of avoiding pending misfortune.

Minding your Ps and Qs

As a warning to watch how you behave it's possible that 'minding your Ps and Qs' originated in the genteel surroundings of the French court in the seventeenth century. There dancing instructors would caution their pupils to mind their *pieds* (feet) and *queues* (tails of their wigs) when they took to the floor. On such occasions dancers who bowed their heads too low when making formal bows risked losing their tall elaborate wigs which were liable to slip off their heads and cause considerable embarrassment. Nearer home, 'Ps and Qs' have also been linked to the practice of publicans who kept an account of how much

beer their customers drank by marking pints under 'P' and quarts (two pints) under 'Q'. Customers were well advised to keep a check on their 'Ps and Qs' to avoid being overcharged when it came to the final reckoning.

Monkey up the chimney

If a householder had 'a monkey up the chimney' he had a mortgage. 'Monkey' was, and still is, a slang term for five hundred pounds. The alternative expression for a mortgage was, to have 'a monkey with a long tail'.

Nail drives out nail

It is quite common for a new nail to be used as a punch to drive an old nail out of a piece of timber. This process of expelling something, or someone, of long standing with a new replacement has many resonances in life and the phrase has become a well-established proverb.

Nailing your colours to the mast

Military or naval flags ('colours') are hoisted to the top of a flagpole and secured in place by lines. However, these are vulnerable to being shot away in battle, which could be demoralizing especially as lowering your colours was a signal of surrender. To avoid this risk, 'colours' could be nailed to the mast, an act which also ensured that they could not be lowered in submission and defeat. Therefore, 'nailing your colours to the mast' shows the intention of fighting on to the bitter end.

Neither fish nor fowl

Something that is neither one thing nor another and so is useless to all, is referred to as being 'neither fish nor fowl'. The full expression is 'neither fish, flesh (or fowl), nor good red herring'. The expression dates from the Middle Ages when specific foods were indicative of the various classes of society. Fish was food for the clergy, flesh (or fowl) was the sustenance of the common man, and red herrings were the fare of paupers.

Nest egg

Money laid by acts as an inducement to make further savings, helping the reserve to grow. Referring to this saving as a nest egg alludes to the common practice of placing an egg in a hen's nest to encourage her to lay. The implication in the expression is that even a small sum of money put away stimulates larger savings.

Never choose your women or linen by candlelight

The sound advice contained in this proverb was appreciated in the mid-sixteenth century. It suggests that the decisions concerning the two most important elements of a man's life should be made in broad daylight, rather than in the flattering glow of a candle flame.

New wine in old bottles

Any experienced butler would tell you that to put 'new wine in old bottles' would be unwise, and in fact flies in the face of biblical wisdom. In Matthew 9:17 it says: 'Neither do men put new wine into old bottles: else the bottles break, and the wine runneth out, and the bottles perish.' Figuratively, the expression refers to the introduction of new ideas into an organization that cannot assimilate them.

Nine days' wonder

The origin of this phrase commonly used to describe something that causes a short-lived sensation before being quickly forgotten may lie in the proverb 'A wonder lasts nine days and then the puppy's eyes are open'. The reference here is to the fact that puppies are born blind and cannot see until they are nine days old, just as people can be temporarily 'blinded' by some 'wonder' until they finally see through it and the 'wonder' ceases to interest them.

Nineteen to the dozen

These days 'nineteen to the dozen' is generally used to describe someone who cannot stop talking. However, the sense of ceaseless activity came into being from the early days of steam engines, notably those used to power pumps in mines. A steam engine going 'nineteen to the dozen' was pumping 19,000 gallons of water for every twelve bushels of coal it burned. Far from describing a somewhat wasteful activity, which may be the case today, it was originally a measure of efficiency.

No names, no pack-drill

This phrase, conveying refusal to identify people in order to prevent the possible apportionment of blame, recalls an obsolete army punishment known as 'pack-drill', which involved marching up and down in full marching order. Figuratively the expression means that it is impossible to slander or libel someone whose name is unknown.

Not until the cows come home

Cattle let out to pasture only come back to the farmyard and the dairy when the next milking is due and even then their return can often be a long-winded process.

From this experience in the fields, 'not until the cows come home' carries the sense of something taking a very long time indeed, possibly not happening at all, coupled with an air of indolence and procrastination.

Not worth a rush

Long before carpets were invented, rushes were strewn to provide floor covering. In medieval homes, the rushes were renewed or replaced if an important guest was expected.

Someone who was not considered worthy of such an honour would have to put up with used rushes or none at all. Figuratively the expression came to be used to describe something or someone considered worthless.

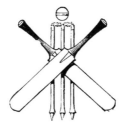

On a sticky wicket

Weather conditions play an important part in games of cricket, especially those in the British Isles. Given that the ball is almost always bowled so that it bounces on the wicket before reaching the player who is batting, the condition of the wicket is of vital importance in deciding what tactics to employ. A 'sticky wicket' is one of the most hazardous to play on. Rain-soaked, but fast-drying, it can make the ball break sharply and rise abruptly. Batting on a 'sticky wicket' requires concentration and skill, to avoid accidentally mistiming a stroke and thereby presenting a catch to the fielding side, or allowing the ball to hit the wicket. The phrase is used less frequently away from the cricket field than it once was. However, its wider meaning remains the same, implying that care and vigilance are needed in dealing with an awkward and unpredictable situation.

On the nail

The nail referred to in this saying from the medieval market place resembles the shape of a carpenter's nail, though it is a great deal bigger. The nail in the market was a stand topped by a shallow vessel which formed the focal point for market trading. Vendors would place a sample of their goods, frequently grain, in the vessel where they would be inspected by potential purchasers. If the purchasers were satisfied with the quality and price of what was being offered to them, they would seal the bargain by placing their payment in the vessel as well; in other words paying 'on the nail'.

From medieval markets use of the term widened to the point where paying 'on the nail' implies immediate payment for goods or services.

On your beam ends

To be on one's beam ends is to be in serious trouble, much as a wooden ship was considered to be in a desperate predicament when the wind and sea forced it to heel right over on its side.

Such ships had large wooden beams running across the framework from side to side. They supported the decks and held the sides together. To be on the 'beam ends' then, was to be heeling over at an alarming angle.

Out of the top drawer

Maybe because it was often, literally, the place in a chest of drawers where you kept your most favoured possessions, in its figurative sense the term came to represent 'the best', as well the 'upper class'. In time the expression widened to include 'the hankie drawer' – again referring to the top drawer of a chest where such small items were stored, but this time it being used in particular reference to the higher echelons of society. In a disparaging way someone would be referred to as 'not being out of the hankie drawer', that is to say he was not a born member of the upper classes.

Over-egg the pudding

The danger of putting too much of any ingredient into a dish is a 'recipe for disaster', and in the case of eggs it is no exception. In a non-literal sense, 'to over-egg the pudding' means to wildly exaggerate or overstate your case, which in a figurative sense could also be another 'recipe for disaster'.

Over the mahogany

A rich and strong wood, mahogany was first brought to England from the West Indies as ships' ballast and it was not until the 1750s that it began to be imported in large quantities for making furniture – dining tables in particular. If a man said he was going to discuss something 'over the mahogany', it meant he was planning to discuss a subject with his wife over dinner. The expression, in northern homes, became 'with the mahogany', and so 'mahogany' became a slang word for wife. 'Under the mahogany', on the other hand, was not where a husband longed to be, but was slang for a friendly gathering or social occasion; and 'to decorate the mahogany' was to put money on the bar for a round of drinks in a pub.

Painting the king's picture

Among criminals 'painting the king's picture' is a euphemism for forging money. In days gone by this applied particularly to coins, since most coins carried the monarch's head on one side.

Passing the buck

These days, 'passing the buck' means evading responsibility or shifting blame onto other people. When the phrase was coined in the nineteenth century, however, it had a different emphasis. In some card games a marker, known as a 'buck', was placed in front of the dealer to show who the dealer was. When it was someone else's turn to deal, the 'buck' was passed. Originally the 'buck' may have been a piece of buck-shot, or possibly a silver dollar, which was passed from dealer to dealer.

Paying through the nose

Various theories are put forward to explain the origin of this graphic expression for anyone forced to pay more for something than it is really worth. One explanation links it with a form of early taxation imposed by Danish invaders, who punished those who refused to pay by slitting their noses. Another draws an analogy between a bleeding nose and someone who is 'bled' by being obliged to pay an excessive price.

Pearls before swine

In St Matthew's gospel, the reference to what became this well known proverb runs:

> Give not that which is holy unto the dogs, neither cast ye your pearls before swine, lest they trample them under their feet, and turn again and rend you.

Whether the pearls described are pearls of wisdom or pearls in any other figurative sense, the caution is the same, warning against offering anything of quality to those incapable of appreciating and valuing it.

Peppercorn rent

Nominal rents of negligible value are sometimes paid by tenants who are allowed to occupy premises owned by others almost free of charge. These are referred to. as 'peppercorn rents' since a peppercorn, though of very little value, still represents a financial exchange between tenant and landlord. This is important as it confirms the owner's ultimate rights to the property.

Pidgin English

Although this trading language is sometimes spelt 'pigeon English', 'pidgin' is the correct form, for the word approximates to a Chinese speaker's pronunciation of the English word 'business'. Pidgin English developed as a means of communication along the coast of China after English ships began trading there from the seventeenth century onwards. Although an artificial language, it proved to be a successful means of conducting business between speakers of English and Chinese, incorporating as it does elements from both. Pidgin Englishes have developed for similar reasons in other parts of the world with equal success. In one instance they have found their way back to the UK where the expression 'That's my pidgin (pigeon)' means 'That's my business'.

Pie in the sky

When this phrase was popularized in the early years of the twentieth century it formed part of a trenchant political and social message. In 1911 a militant Trade Union song book, *Songs of the Workers*, was published and included among its titles 'The Preacher and the Slave' by Joe Hill, which contained the verse:

> You will eat, by and by,
> In that glorious land above the sky;
> Work and pray, live on hay,
> You'll get pie in the sky when you die.

Since then 'pie in the sky' has meant the 'good time' or the 'good things' that are promised but which never come, or are never realized.

Pig and whistle

This unlikely pairing which is used as the name for many English public houses is in all likelihood the corrupt spelling of two Old English words, *piggin* and *wassail*. The first of these was an earthenware container from which drinkers filled their own mugs and *wassail* was a traditional greeting used when drink was offered to a guest or when a toast was drunk to his health. Put together the *piggin* and *wassail* seem an ideal combination for a public house: it's only the changes in spelling that have obscured their origins and given pub sign-painters endless scope for their creative powers.

Pig in a poke

A 'pig in a poke' is a blind bargain, that is to say one entered into without the purchaser knowing for sure what it is that he or she is buying. The saying dates from the time when live sucking pigs were offered for sale at markets. A common trick played by unscrupulous traders was to display one pig and offer others for sale conveniently tied up in bags. Only purchasers who had the sense to look inside the bag before handing over their money could be certain of what they were buying. Those who paid first and only checked later could well discover that they had bought a relatively worthless cat or puppy.

And why 'poke'? From the thirteenth century 'poke' was the word for a bag or small sack, derived from the French *poche*, from which we get 'pouch' and 'pocket' in English.

Pigs in clover

The image of 'pigs in clover' is one of unbridled plenty and comfort, a field of succulent clover on which pigs can graze to their hearts' content.

The reference to pigs carries a note of mild disapproval though, when the pigs refer to other people. Here the inference is that some well-fed, in other words well-to-do, people may find themselves leading a life of well-endowed comfort without appreciating how to conduct themselves appropriately.

Pinning your heart on your sleeve

The world of the Middle Ages is recalled in this chivalrous reference to knights who went into a tournament wearing a token of their lady's. In modern times those who make their affections apparent for all the world to see are said to have 'pinned their hearts on their sleeves'.

Plain as a pikestaff

Although pikestaffs measuring sixteen feet in length are not commonly seen today, they were familiar and unmistakable objects in the sixteenth century when they were the principal weapons of the foot soldiers known as pikemen. In spite of this historical lapse, anything described as being 'as plain as a pikestaff' is still as blindingly obvious today as it would have been four hundred years ago.

Plough the headland before the butts

This might be said of the country dweller who starts something at the wrong end. The 'headland' was the strip of land left unploughed at either end of a field on which the plough turns. The headlands are only ploughed when ploughing the rest of the field has been completed.

Poker to draw up a fire

In the days when evil spirits and hobgoblins were the dread of common folk and lords alike, it was believed that to place the poker across the front of the grate with its point towards the chimney would make the fire draw. In reality the action had no effect whatsoever on the efficiency of the fire but created the shape of the Cross, against which all spirits are helpless. The primary concern was to keep the house spirit, Lob, at bay, as he was inclined to lie by the fire and instigate mischievous pranks.

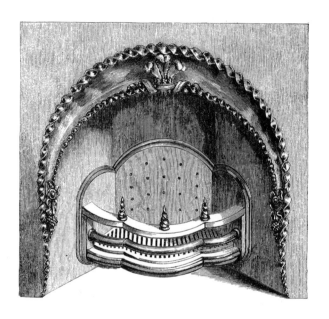

Pulling a fast one

'Pulling a fast one' generally implies that some underhand method has been used to deceive and possibly cheat another person. However, when the phrase was coined in cricket it represented a perfectly legitimate ploy used by bowlers. Changing the speed at which a ball is bowled is one way of confusing the player batting at the other end and possibly catching him or her unawares. Bowlers who vary the pace of their deliveries, as well as their direction, are more likely to take wickets than those whose bowling becomes predictable. So, 'pulling a fast one' in a cricketing context means 'bowling an unexpectedly fast ball'.

Pulling the chestnuts out of the fire

Since the Middle Ages 'pulling the chestnuts out of the fire' has been used in the sense of retrieving a difficult situation for someone, often by extricating them from an embarrassment.

The allusion in the saying is to the old fable of the monkey and the cat. The monkey discovers chestnuts roasting in the embers of a fire and decides he would like to eat them. However, removing the chestnuts from the fire would risk burning his paws, so the monkey persuades his friend the cat to use his paws to pull the chestnuts from the fire for him.

Pull the wool over someone's eyes

This expression meaning 'to deceive' comes from the days when wigs were the fashion. They were commonly known as 'wool' because of the resemblance to a sheep's fleece, especially wigs with tight curls. Therefore, to pull the wool over someone's eyes would be to stop them seeing what was happening around them.

Put a sock in it

This impolite way of asking someone to quieten down is said to come from the days of wind-up gramophones, where the sound came out through a horn. In lieu of a volume control, it was said that a sock was the most efficient way of muffling the sound.

Putting the cart before the horse

'Putting the cart before the horse', so that the animal pushes rather than draws the cart, is a reversal of the natural order that has probably been used as a metaphor for getting things back to front and in the wrong sequence, for as long as horses have been used as draught animals.

The proverb is known in many languages, though in French and Italian oxen are quoted in place of the horse found in the English and German versions.

Putting the kibosh on

To 'put the kibosh on' something is to put an end to it once and for all. Various origins have been suggested. One traces a link with a Yiddish word, *kabas*, meaning 'to suppress'. Another looks to a hunting term used in Scotland, *caboche*, which is the process of cutting off a deer's head close behind the horns. There is also an Irish *cie bais*, in which the second word is pronounced 'bosh'. This is translated as 'cap of death'. Whichever explanation is chosen, they all have a sense of finality.

Pyrrhic victory

In 279 BC Pyrrhus, King of Epirus, led a sizeable army against the Romans at the Battle of Asculum. Although his forces won, the cost in casualties was so great that Pyrrhus has been remembered for his comment, 'One more such victory and we are lost.' Since that time the term 'Pyrrhic victory' has been given to all successes that have been so costly they amounted to defeats.

Rain before seven, fine before eleven

A respected rhyme, which is frequently confirmed by the improvement in the weather that follows a damp start to the day.

Raining cats and dogs

According to Norse mythology the cat was closely associated with the weather; in fact witches were believed to disguise themselves as cats when they rode on storm clouds. Dogs too had connections with clouds through their status as attendants on Odin, the god of storms. Together they represented the torrential rain and fierce wind that characterized the weather when it 'rained cats and dogs'.

Raising the wind

Just as a sailing ship cannot make headway without wind to fill the sails and drive her forward, so many business enterprises cannot proceed without borrowed capital. In this context 'wind' is a euphemism for money and 'raising the wind' means 'raising money'.

Red herring

Understanding the origin of this familiar expression is not helped by the fact that only half of it is generally used today.

Most of us accept that a 'red herring' represents anything that is used to divert attention from the principal issue that is being investigated or considered. However, the significance of the saying only becomes clear when we discover that the full wording is 'drawing a red herring across the path'.

The herring in this case was much like a kipper: dried, smoked and salted. Drawn across the path taken by a fox, it would cover the animal's scent and divert pursuing hounds into following a false trail.

Red-letter day

'Red-letter days' are days to be looked forward to and remembered with special pleasure. In bygone days saints' days and important Christian feast days were printed in red ink in the church calendar to distinguish them from other days in the church year which were printed in black.

Red sky at night, shepherd's delight; red sky in the morning, shepherd's warning

This is probably the most frequently quoted saying of weather lore and, like many such sayings, there is more to it than rural whimsy and old wives' tales. Indeed, this particular observation draws on biblical authority: when St Matthew describes the occasion when the Pharisees taunted Christ to show them a sign from heaven. He, in reply, told them: 'When it is evening, ye say, it will be fair weather: for the sky is red. And in the morning, it will be foul weather today: for the sky is red and lowering. O ye hypocrites, ye can discern the face of the sky; but can ye not discern the signs of the times?'

Riding a hobby-horse

In time the hobby-horse became widely known as a children's toy made from a stick topped by a horse's head, across which the child straddled. However, this was a simplified model of the far more elaborate and much older hobby-horse that first accompanied Morris dancers in their May Day celebrations to welcome the arrival of spring. These original hobby-horses comprised a light wickerwork frame draped with appropriately decorated cloths.

In either case a hobby-horse became synonymous with something to which an individual was strongly attached. In time this attachment took on an obsessive nature, so that 'riding a hobby-horse' or 'getting on a hobby-horse' came to mean talking at length about a pet project or theory, to the point at which others begin to tire of hearing about it.

Riding roughshod over

Those in the habit of 'riding roughshod over' others act with complete disregard for their feelings or interests. The expression originated among battlefield cavalry units of days gone by, in which horses were sometimes fitted with special shoes with sharp projections and cutting edges. These were intended to add further terror to the foot-soldiers against whom they went into action and who would suffer terribly from being ridden over by 'roughshod' cavalry.

Right-hand man

As the senior assistant a 'right-hand man' was accorded pride of place over other servants and traditionally this was on his master's right-hand side. In this position he was better placed to fend off attack with the use of his sword. And occupying a position of such importance he was as indispensable to his master as his own right hand.

Ringing the changes

In traditional English bell-ringing changes are rung using all the combinations of a set of bells. This is extended into everyday speech as an allusion to re-using the same limited resources in a variety of inventive ways.

Robbing Peter to pay Paul

Peter and Paul have been seen as contrasting figures since early Christian times and there are no specific references to any particular Peter or Paul in this widely-used saying. The meaning is plain: there is no point in paying off one debt if doing so means incurring another.

Rod in pickle

Having 'a rod in pickle' means to have an unpleasant surprise in store for someone. The allusion is to corporal punishment, which was once a regular feature of education and chastisement in general. Birch rods used to administer such a beating were kept in brine (pickle) to ensure that the twigs remained supple.

Run the gauntlet

To 'run the gauntlet' is to be criticized and attacked on all sides. The expression appeared in English during the Thirty Years War in the first half of the seventeenth century. When it was first used 'gauntlet' was spelt *gantlope*, a Swedish word formed from *gata* ('a lane') and *lopp* ('a course'). This referred to a punishment current in the Swedish armed forces in which those sentenced were made to pass between the crew or company drawn up in two lines forming a narrow gap between them. Armed with rope ends, or other appropriate weapons, every man in the line beat the miscreant, while he 'ran the gauntlet'.

Salt of the earth

Salt was a vital commodity in the ancient world. Roman soldiers received part of their pay as a *salarium*, an allowance with which they bought salt; the English word 'salary' is derived from this.

Salt was used to preserve food as well as season it, and the saying 'salt of the earth' received its ultimate endorsement when Christ used the term to describe his disciples in the Sermon on the Mount: 'Ye are the salt of the earth: but if the salt have lost his savour, wherewith shall it be salted? It is thenceforth good for nothing, but to be cast out, and to be trodden under the foot of men.'

From this point on, anyone described as the salt of the earth could reasonably regard themselves as among the best of mankind.

Salt on his tail

It was once believed that if you wanted to catch a bird, you needed to put salt on its tail.

Whatever the truth of this, the idea became well enough established for putting 'salt on his tail' to become a euphemism for apprehending a felon.

Save your bacon

There are two ideas about why this expression conveys the idea of saving oneself from injury or harm. The first is based on the importance of 'bacon' as the principal meat that was salted and preserved for the lean winter months. Undoubtedly, the diligent housewife would take steps to prevent such a store being tampered with, or raided, to ensure her family was catered for until spring. However, the second explanation is based on the idea that the Anglo-Saxon word for 'back' was *baec*, which was also the Old Dutch word for 'bacon'. Therefore to 'save your bacon', it is thought, was to literally save your back from a thrashing.

Scooping the pool

'Scooping the pool' means winning all the money staked in a gambling game and by analogy to be 'totally successful' in any other venture. 'Pool' has an interesting history when used in this and similar expressions. Although spelt differently, it is derived from the French *poule*, meaning a hen. This may be because hens were once set as the target or prize in games, as in the old *jeu de la poule* ('game of the hen').

Send to Coventry

This well-known phrase seems to derive from the particular dislike the people of Coventry had at one time for soldiers. During the English Civil War, Royalist soldiers captured in Warwickshire were sent to the Parliamentary stronghold of Coventry, where the citizens made it plain what they thought of them and their cause. It was also said that any woman in Coventry seen talking to a soldier was immediately ostracized by her townsfolk. No doubt attitudes in Coventry have changed

radically since those times, but the expression is still used as a term for humiliating a person by completely ignoring him or her.

Setting the Thames on fire

This phrase is usually used in the negative, as in 'He'll never set the Thames on fire', meaning 'He'll never make much of a mark in life'. It has been in use since the eighteenth century, but the principal rivers of other countries have been used in a similar context for longer and all the sayings share a common meaning.

Settling on the lees

Lees occur in wine making in the form of sediment that collects at the bottom of a barrel or bottle. As such they are the dregs that are thrown away after the wine has been removed.

Anyone obliged to settle on the lees, is forced to resort to settling down on what is left after the best has gone, in other words to making do with what is left after the main part of one's resources have been consumed, often recklessly.

Set your cap at someone

For 'cap' you can read hat or bonnet and one school of thought suggests that it relates to the wearing of beguiling or alluring headgear with a view to impressing a man. Certainly it means trying to win someone's favour; but another idea is that it has nothing to do with headgear at all but comes from a French nautical term, *mettre le cap sur*, meaning to head towards or steer for. Whatever its origin, the expression was in use in the early nineteenth century.

Sew pillows under people's elbows

While to 'sew pillows under people's elbows' sounds like a Heath Robinson idea of comfort, the expression actually dates from the fourteenth-century Wycliffe Bible. It means to give someone a false sense of security. The expression gained favour again in the seventeenth century, thanks to the use of it by the Restoration playwright, William Wycherley, who was famed for his bawdy works.

Shoeing the goose

Just about the last thing that a goose needs is to have shoes attached to its feet like a horse, and that is the point of this apparently ridiculous notion.

'Shoeing the goose' is an absurd idea, not to mention a complete waste of time. The implication in the saying is the warning that time can be frittered away on trifles rather than concentrating on things that really need to be done

Shooting your bolt

In medieval archery a 'bolt' was the short blunt arrow fired from a crossbow. Although powerful and accurate, crossbows were cumbersome weapons to reload and as a result had a far slower rate of fire than the longbow. With only one bolt to shoot at a time, an archer who had shot his bolt had nothing with which to attack (or possibly defend himself) until he reloaded the next. From this we get the present-day meaning of 'shooting your bolt', to have tried your utmost, expending all your resources, but to no avail.

Show the white feather

This expression which symbolizes cowardice dates from the time when cock fighting was a popular national pastime. Since no pure-bred gamecock had any white feathers in its plumage, a bird with even a single white feather showed itself up as being of inferior stock and therefore unlikely to show the fighting characteristics of a thoroughbred. White feathers became a token of cowardice and during the First World War, men of fighting age who were seen wearing civilian clothes were liable to be handed white feathers by women who thought that they should be in uniform fighting for their country. The inference behind this was presumably that men who were not members of the armed forces must have been cowards.

Sleep like a top

It is often said that when you sleep deeply and soundly you 'sleep like a top'. Commonly, the allusion is put down to the seeming momentary pause of a spinning top when its rotation is at its height. However, there is another, rather more plausible explanation. The Italians have a saying that expresses the idea of a deep and peaceful slumber: '*Ei dorme come un topo*'. Translated it means 'he sleeps like a mouse'. *Topo* is the generic name and the Italian expression relates to the dormouse, that most somnolent of mice.

Soft soap

That 'soft soap' can be used as a term for flattery, is a reflection of the luxurious froth and bubbles such soap creates. The more common soap was made of a mixture of vegetable or animal fats and 'lye', a strong alkaline solution often made from the ashes of the household fire. Such soap was reasonably efficient but harsh on the skin and those who could afford it bought soaps imported from Venice and Spain, particularly the fine white soap of Castile.

Soul above buttons

We must all surely have heard someone referred to as having 'ideas above his station'. In Victorian times to have one's 'soul above buttons' was the reverse notion. Someone who was considered to have his 'soul above buttons' was someone who actually was, or was presumed to be, superior to the position he held.

Sowing wild oats

In agricultural terms wild oats are weeds: poor quality cereals as opposed to the richer yielding crop of cultivated oats. On some farms wild oats have been hand-weeded from fields of growing corn well into modern times.

To sow wild oats, then, is to undertake a reckless and frankly wasteful course of action and it has long been used with reference to young people (invariably young men) who 'sow wild oats' by indulging in the final excesses of youth before they settle down to lead mature and profitable lives.

Spare at the spigot and spoil at the bung

A 'spigot' is a small peg which is inserted into the vent hole of a barrel or cask, the allusion here being to one filled with a valuable liquid such as beer or wine.

As a metaphor, this saying points to the owner's meanness over small things. By taking excessive care not to waste any of the barrel's valuable contents at the vent hole, he overlooks the main bung sealing the barrel, through which his drink is leaking in profusion.

To 'spare at the spigot and spoil at the bung' therefore means to be tight-fisted about things that don't matter, while being wasteful when it comes to those which really are important.

Spick and span

The original version of this phrase was 'spick and span new' and like many others in this collection it came from the world of ships and shipping in which a *spic* was a nail or spike used in ship-building and a *span* was a chip of wood. New ships that had come straight from the shipyard contained shiny new nails and tell-tale wood chips left from the carpenters' work. Since those days the meaning has altered somewhat. The association with newness has been replaced with a broader sense of being neat, tidy and well-presented.

Spiking his guns

In the early days of field artillery, the charge which propelled the ball or other projectile from the barrel was detonated by igniting its gunpowder through a small touch-hole. If a metal spike was driven in to block this touch-hole, the gun could not be fired and was rendered useless. From this act of battlefield sabotage 'spiking his guns' has been given a wider application, referring to any action that foils an opponent's plans.

Spilling the beans

'Spilling the beans' is the inadvertent divulging of information which would otherwise have been kept secret. One explanation places the origin of the phrase in ancient Greece, where it was customary for beans of two different colours to be used in secret ballots, held among members of an organization to which a would-be member was applying. Those in favour of his joining voted with a white bean, signifying 'yes'; a brown bean counted as a 'no' vote. When all votes had been cast, the beans were counted in secret, so that the prospective member would have no idea how many votes there were for and against him. The only way he could discover this was if the beans were accidentally spilt in his presence. Another line of thought follows the idea that some fortune-tellers use beans instead of crystal balls or tea leaves. They rely instead on spilling beans from a cup and then interpreting the future from the pattern made by them.

Splicing the mainbrace

In the Royal Navy the order to 'splice the mainbrace' signals the very rare allocation of an extra tot of rum ('grog') to a ship's company. The expression has been used since the early years of the nineteenth century and probably originates from the provision of an extra ration of rum to the seamen who succeeded in the difficult and arduous task of splicing (repairing and joining) the 'mainbrace', the rope attached to the yard from which the mainsail hung. Since the days of sailing ships 'splicing the mainbrace' has become a general euphemism for having a drink.

Spoilt as a lace tablecloth

The time and devotion it takes to make fine, hand-made lace has ensured it has always been a costly commodity. The allusion in this simile is to the care that was lavished on such a tablecloth, storing it carefully and using it only on special occasions. To be looked after equally well would be to be pampered indeed. Since the introduction of machine-made lace in the mid-nineteenth century this expression has rather lost its pertinence. Prior to that lace making was a major industry in Britain and in the later stages of the eighteenth century about a hundred thousand people were employed in it.

D TODD

Square meal

There is no definite evidence to explain where this phrase originates. However, it has been suggested that it comes from the predecessors of an essential item of crockery. Long before plates as we know them were in common use, food was served on trenchers. These were made from square-cut slices of stale brown bread hollowed out in the centre. A wealthy man would have several trenchers for his use during a meal, the more humble only one or two. At the end of the meal the trenchers would be gathered up and given to the poor. In time, wood took over from bread. The new-look trencher was a square of wood, again with a large hollow in the centre but with the addition of a small hollow in one corner for salt. If plentiful, the food would be piled into the centre of the square thus providing a full and satisfying meal.

Stalking horse

Horses were not always used in the hunt to pursue game. At one time hunters were accustomed to dismount and hide behind their mounts, which moved steadily towards the quarry until the hunters were within aim. In time actual horses were replaced by artificial horses that amounted to a hide-cum-decoy.

The sense of concealment used to gain closer access to a goal, was taken up in the political arena during the nineteenth century, when a 'stalking horse' became a candidate who was put forward in an election to test the water for another and, potentially, far more successful candidate. In British politics a 'stalking horse' has been used to challenge for the leadership of political parties. The candidate in question has had no realistic chance of winning the election. His role has been to gauge the weight of support for a challenge to the current leader and to reveal how well stronger candidates might fare in a leadership contest.

Stitch in time

One of the most familiar of all English proverbs, 'a stitch in time saves nine' is used to suggest that prompt action now will save undue work in the future. There have been various sermons and treatises applauding the wisdom of the saying, including one by a Noah Webster, who in his work *The prompter; or Common Sayings, and subjects, which are full of common sense*, published in 1808, is adamant that:

'. . . in no article does a "stitch in time" save so much as in government. One public officer neglects his duty a little, another cheats a little, but these peccadilloes are overlooked; the mischief is not great . . . until at last a thousand little evils swell into a great public one.'

Straight from the horse's mouth

The only sure way of establishing the age of a horse is to examine its front teeth. This has always provided incontrovertible proof, so much so that 'straight from the horse's mouth' became

synonymous with the most senior and highly respected source on any given subject.

Swinging the lead

Aboard ship it used to be the task of the leadsman to find the depth of water in which his ship was sailing by casting a lead weight attached to a measuring line ahead of the vessel and noting how much line disappeared below the surface. Lazy leadsmen merely went through the motions by swinging the lead and this, like many nautical expressions, has come ashore as a term to describe shirking any activity by making up a plausible excuse or feigning illness.

Take it in snuff

The 'snuff' in this metaphor is not the powdered tobacco that became very fashionable during, and after, the Restoration (Queen Anne was even a devotee), but the 'snuff' of a candle, the burnt out and smoky end of the wick. To 'take it in snuff' meant to take offence or be in a huff.

Take with a pinch of salt

This expression, which has been in common use since the mid-seventeenth century comes directly from the Latin 'cum grano selis'. It is used to advise against wholly believing any extravagant or inaccurate claim. It suggests that taking a grain of salt with something will make it easier to swallow and more palatable.

Taking a rain check

'Rain checks' entered general usage by way of sporting events in America. These were usually baseball games, in which a 'rain check' was a ticket which permitted the holder to be re-admitted to the game after it had had to be postponed because of rain. In the last fifty years the term has broadened to mean a 'deferment'. 'Let's take a rain check on that' means 'let's put that on hold for the time being'. It is also used as an acceptance of an invitation for a later date, as in 'I'll take a rain check on that', meaning 'I'm sorry I can't come on this occasion, but please invite me next time'.

Taking down a peg

There was once a strict hierarchy at sea displayed by the position of ship's colours after they had been raised. The greatest honour was conferred by flags flown at the top of the mast. The flags, and therefore the degree of honour they bestowed, could be lowered by pegs. To be 'taken down a peg' was to receive a reduction in the honour shown to you. This nautical practice has developed a metaphorical use for taking the conceit from a boastful or 'stuck-up' person.

Taking pot luck

When most household cooking took place over an open fire the
majority of meals were prepared in a large cooking pot that was
kept boiling over the fire. This contained everything that was to
be consumed in the meal: vegetables, cereals and, on occasion,
a small amount of meat. With catering of this sort, a meal from

the pot comprised whatever had been put into the pot to cook and 'taking pot luck' amounted to offering visitors the opportunity to join the family meal and share whatever happened to be in the pot at that time.

This was in contrast to preparing a special meal for visitors in advance and 'taking pot luck' retains its original meaning even though cooking pots have been replaced by modern domestic cookers and microwaves. Anyone invited to 'take pot luck' shares in whatever the family is going to eat, without any special provision for visitors.

Taking the biscuit

To 'take the biscuit' can be interpreted in two ways, depending whether it is being used ironically or not. As a straightforward statement of approbation, 'taking the biscuit' means being 'the best of the lot', even 'being incredible'. However, it is commonly used to express a strong degree of irony, in expressions like, 'I've heard some daft things in my time, but that takes the biscuit!' 'Taking the biscuit' is an Anglicized form of an expression common in America from the middle of the nineteenth century. The American expression refers to 'taking the cake', an allusion to the cake awarded to the winners of a 'cakewalk'. This was a nineteenth-century pastime, popular with Black Americans, in which couples walked arm in arm around a room. The couple judged to be the most graceful walkers 'took the cake' as their prize.

Taking the chair

Dining chairs, as we know them, did not become popular until the mid-sixteenth century. Prior to that, the most common form of seating was the bench and the settle. Most homes would have only one, or maybe two, individual chairs with arms and backs and these were for the use of the most important persons. Hence, the most distinguished visitor would be invited to 'take the chair' and could be described as the 'chairman'.

Taking the gilt off the gingerbread

To counteract the dull, dark appearance of gingerbread, there was a time when ginger cakes were gilded with a thin layer of real gold leaf, or Dutch leaf – which looked like gold – to make them appear more appetising. These golden delights were popular fairground fare but once the gilt was removed the cake could be seen for what it really was. In time the expression became synonymous for showing something to be less valuable than initial appearances would suggest, or for destroying an illusion.

Talking turkey

This expression originated in America where it was in common usage by the middle of the nineteenth century, before spreading throughout the English-speaking world. 'Talking turkey' means 'talking business', or 'talking seriously'. It appears to date from the early days of the colonies, when turkeys formed an important part of the trade between the native Indians and the Pilgrim Fathers. Before long the Indians realized that every trading visit would involve their supplying turkeys and 'You come to talk turkey?' became a familiar saying whenever a colonist appeared to discuss business.

Tarred with the same brush

The metaphorical action of 'tarring with the same brush', is to condemn someone, or a group of people, for the same reason that you condemn others, whether that condemnation is justified or not. The saying stems from the use of tar by shepherds in earlier times. Cuts and other sores on the skin of sheep used to be treated by a dab with a brush dipped in tar. Once all the sheep had been treated, all had been 'tarred with the same brush', in other words they had all been treated in the same way without distinction or discrimination.

The balloon's gone up

The start of excitement or action is vividly encapsulated in this phrase which dates from the First World War, when often the first sign of an action beginning was the launching of a balloon. These could be signal balloons, commanding gunners along the front to begin firing, or balloons carrying aloft observers to direct an attack. Either way, to the troops in the trenches, word that 'the balloon's gone up' meant that action of some form was imminent.

The cup that cheers

The reference is to tea and comes from a quotation from William Cowper who in 1785 in *The Task* wrote:

> And, while the bubbling and loud-hissing urn
> Throws up a steamy column, and the cups,
> That cheer but not inebriate, wait on each.

The devil to pay and no pitch hot

Here is another nautical expression with a specific meaning. The 'devil' was a seam on board wooden-hulled ships that was hard to get at and always required more pitch than any other when the gaps in the hull were being sealed to make it watertight. The expression has come down to us meaning that serious trouble is likely to arise as a result of whatever has happened.

The game's not worth the candle

The allusion here is to gambling at cards by candlelight. In this expression the game has reached the point where there is so little money to be won that it does not even amount to the price of a fresh candle that would enable it to be continued. Therefore anything described as not being 'worth the candle' is not worth either the trouble or expense involved in doing it.

The mill cannot grind with the water that is past

This old proverb dates from a time when water mills ground much of the flour in England. Once water had flowed past the

mill, it could not be brought back to turn the mill a second time. The implication of the saying, self-evidently, is that you need to seize opportunities when they are presented, because once they have moved beyond you they cannot be retrieved.

The moon and the weather change together

Scientific investigation in the last fifty years has established what country people have been aware of for thousands of years: that the weather changes with the moon.

One study of the relationship between night-time temperature and the phases of the moon established that there was a regular drop in the minimum night-time temperature for several nights around the time of a full moon.

Similar studies from around the world show the same correlation. One investigation into weather patterns in the USA showed that the phase of the moon could account for nearly 65 per cent of the changes in rainfall and results of a similar magnitude were demonstrated from a weather survey held in Australia.

As Sir Bernard Lovell, the distinguished astronomer, wrote in the mid-1960s, the links between moon phase and the weather appeared to suggest that 'we are moving through a series of scientific fantasies to a proof of ancient beliefs'.

The rotten apple injures its neighbour

At the heart of this and similar proverbs and sayings involving rotten apples is the fact that allowing apples to come into contact with each other risks letting the disease in a rotten apple spread to others. This is why traditional wooden apple racks are arranged to ensure that apples can be stored on wooden slats, with a safe distance between each one. If an apple does become rotten, it will remain isolated from the others and the rest of the crop will remain free of infection.

When it is used metaphorically, 'a rotten apple' is the term applied to an individual whose presence and influence has a deleterious effect on others, especially anyone who comes into close contact with him or her.

Throw the baby out with the bath water

This saying is a direct translation of a German proverb, and suggests that the valuable and essential item can be lost through indiscriminate or rash change. It was known in England in the early years of the seventeenth century, even though taking a bath then was not an everyday experience. Queen Elizabeth, for example, was said to take a bath once a month 'whether she need it or not', but for many of her subjects taking a bath was an annual event at best. In the poorer households the bath water would be shared, with the various members of the family taking their turn. As large families were not uncommon the water must indeed have been murky by the time the baby was immersed, and one can understand more clearly the basis for the expression.

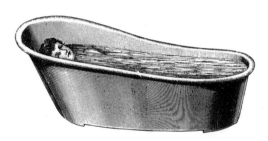

To be put through the mangle

This expression graphically explains having to endure a gruelling experience, to be 'wrung out'. The original con-traptions, the earliest machinery to be used in the laundry, were boxes weighted with stones. These were moved backwards and forwards upon rollers to press sheets, tablecloths and other linen spread flat upon a table beneath. It was not until the nineteenth century that the hand-wringer became fashionable. Two rollers, initially of iron and later of wood, were held with weighted levers or screws to allow the clothes to be passed between them. Hand-operated mangles, in one form or another, were in common use well into the twentieth century when the spin dryer took over the chore.

To have a bone to pick

'To have a bone to pick' with someone means that you have something disagreeable to discuss and settle with them. The allusion is to a bone thrown to dogs, which inevitably leads to snarling and fighting as each tries to win the bone for its own enjoyment.

Too many irons in the fire

Now used to convey the idea that having too many projects on the go inhibits the success of any one of them, the expression comes from the days when irons needed to be heated in or on the fire. Smoothing out the wrinkles from freshly washed and dried clothes and linens was first done by heating up smooth stones in the embers of a fire, and then wrapping them up in a cloth to protect the hands, before pressing them over the fabric. In time, stones were replaced by flat irons, which again were heated on a grid above a fire and later again upon a stove. To save time a busy laundress would heat up several irons simultaneously, but in doing so she risked them getting too hot and scorching or burning the clothes or linens being ironed.

To trail your coat

This was a way, in times long past, when you could literally 'ask for trouble'. The custom was that a man who was feeling quarrelsome or aggressive trailed his coat along the ground, as a way of asking someone to step on it and thus instigate a fight.

Trim someone's lamps

To trim was a synonym for 'to thrash' and your 'lamps' were your eyes in street slang. Therefore to have your 'lamps trimmed' was to receive two black eyes. In its literal sense of course, it was a necessary function to ensure lamp wicks burnt efficiently.

True blue will never stain

A 'true blue' is a person who is constant, loyal, faithful and reliable. Such a person is reckoned never to disgrace himself and the allusion in 'true blue will never stain' is to the blue aprons traditionally worn by butchers, which do not show blood stains.

Turning the corner

Having got over the worst of any setback one can be said to have 'turned the corner'. The corner from which the expression originates is a geographical 'corner'. In fact there are two: The Cape of Good Hope at the southern tip of Africa and Cape Horn at the southern tip of South America. In both cases ships that had sailed round the cape and were now setting sail for the rest of their voyage were said to have 'turned the corner'.

Up corn, down horn

This is an old saying which points to the relative prices paid for corn and beef ('horn') at markets in days gone by. When corn prices were high, the price of beef tended to fall, since buyers had less money to spend on meat.

Upper crust

In days gone by loaves were baked directly on the floor of the oven, and consequently the lower part of the loaf became charred. This was cut off and fed to the menial domestic staff, while the top part, the 'upper crust' was offered to the most important guests. Figuratively it came to be a term for the aristocracy or higher echelons of society.

Use your loaf

In rhyming slang a 'loaf of bread' means a 'head'. This is usually shortened to 'loaf' and telling someone 'use your loaf' means 'use your head, or 'use your brains'.

Watching the wise tree

As far back as Roman times, the mulberry tree was a valuable guide in the spring to the passing of frosts and later to their arrival at the close of autumn. This is due to the fact that the mulberry is probably the most sensitive of our trees. Mulberry leaves do not begin to show until all other trees are bringing forth green buds and even the mildest frost in autumn will set the mulberry shedding its leaves.

In the middle of the nineteenth century a clergyman in Huntingdonshire was told by one of his parishioners that 'the wise tree' had not yet begun to bud: '. . . it isn't like some trees as puts out their leaves early and then gets nipped . . .' explained the parishioner. 'You may rest content on the wise tree telling you when you may be safe against frosses.'

Wet blanket

For centuries, a person whose lack of enthusiasm spoils other people's pleasure or causes social discomfort has been labelled 'a wet blanket' and the expression alludes to the use of a wet blanket to dampen down a fire. The origins of the term 'blanket', however, are more interesting. Originally the name 'blanket' referred to an undyed woollen fabric that was used in a variety of ways. We know the French word *blanc* to mean white, but the English derivation 'blank' could mean just what it says, or white or grey. Perhaps because the fabric was so suitable for the task,

the term blanket came to be used exclusively from the early fourteenth century for the warm bedcover we know it to be. However, it is also claimed that the covers are so named because a Mr Thomas Blanket of Bristol was the first manufacturer of the items. If that is the case, one can but delight in the wonderful coincidence of his surname.

What's sauce for the goose is sauce for the gander

This has often been referred to as 'the woman's proverb', as it calls for equality between men and women. It was first recognized in England in the seventeenth century, but is believed to have a much earlier provenance. As an aside, the traditional sauce for goose is made from apples, as the goose comes to maturity and is fit for killing at the same time as the apple harvest.

Where the shoe pinches

We perhaps know this expression as 'there's the rub', as it means the root cause of any problem. The full saying is 'no one knows where the shoe pinches but the wearer' and it is believed to come directly from the reply of a Roman sage when asked why he was divorcing his beautiful wife. It is said that in response he pulled the shoe from his foot and having gained the questioner's agreement that it was indeed a fine shoe, then asked him to point out where it pinched.

Whistling for it

One thing you can be sure of these days is that if someone says 'You can whistle for it', there is very little chance that you will get what you hope for. This sarcastic tone was not always present. In the days of sailing ships it was popularly believed among sailors that a breeze could literally be 'whistled up' if a ship was becalmed. When something was whistled for then, it was with hope and a strong sense of expectation.

Wide will wear, tight will tear

Just as it is generally accepted that if clothing is too tight it is more prone to tearing, this proverb was said to encourage good measure in government. It was said that if a man's actions were too tightly fettered it would lead to disorder. More moderate restrictions, on the other hand, stood a much better chance of being accepted.

Wild goose chase

Today we use the saying 'wild goose chase' in the sense of a vain pursuit. But the original meaning of 'wild goose chase' dates from a time when a game of follow-my-leader on horseback was popular in rural England. It was called a 'wild goose chase' because the appearance of the riders, evenly spaced one behind the other, resembled the formation of wild geese in flight. In this usage a 'wild goose chase' figuratively represented a rapidly changing course of events which involved quick wits to stay in touch with what was happening.

By the middle of the eighteenth century the modern meaning had replaced the earlier one and a 'wild goose chase' became an absurd enterprise; an impracticable or useless pursuit of an unachievable goal.

Winning hands down

Here is an expression drawn from the world of racing where jockeys, whose mounts are so far ahead of the rest of field that they need no further urging towards the finish, drop their hands and let their horses run home at their own pace. From this easy victory comes the expression that is now applied to any success that is achieved comfortably and without any need to force the pace.

Working up to the collar

This expression comes from the time when horses provided the principal drawing power on and off the road. Draught horses were fitted with heavy horse collars to which were attached the chains or shafts of the plough or vehicle they were pulling. If a

horse was 'working up to the collar', in other words pulling so hard that the collar was fixed firmly round its neck and shoulders, it was pulling well, using great effort. By contrast horses that let their collars hang loose round their necks were not putting in the same amount of effort.

From horse, the saying has transferred to people. Those 'working up to the collar' are deemed to be working with real effort, avoiding any temptation to take things easy.

Wrong side of the bed

When someone gets up in a bad mood, he or she is said to have 'got out of the wrong side of the bed'. On a more literal level, the 'wrong' side was considered to be the left, and to get out on the left side of the bed was to invite misfortune. You only need to remember that our word 'sinister' is the Latin word for 'left', to appreciate the suspicion there was of a left-handed person or the left side of anything. For that reason it also was considered unlucky to put the left foot to the floor first or to put on the left shoe first.

You can take a horse to (the) water but you cannot make him drink

This saying has been recorded in English, in various forms with and without 'the', from the twelfth century.

The inference is clear: there is always a point at which an obstinate or determined individual will refuse to be drawn in a desired direction, no matter how beneficial that may be.